ALIEN-ATED

Alien-ated

Astonishing interviews of Alien Encounters

BRIAN DAFFERN

BHD Publishing

To my wonderful daughter Katherine.

Thank you for always showing me how important faith is and the full power of it.

CONTENTS

~ ~

INTRODUCTION

Belief vs. Proof of Extraterrestrial life

Belief is a powerful influencer. However, it doesn't constitute scientific proof. Many confuse the two and fail to understand that belief is simply an attitude towards a particular issue, not whether the subject is true or false. The UFO (Unidentified Flying Object) and Extraterrestrial phenomenon have existed for centuries. At the time of this writing, the beginning of the third decade of the Twenty-First Century, belief has never been higher. We have seen released videos from the United States Navy and politicians asking for more information on UFOs from the government. In addition, our television stations are filled with more shows on the subject than we can watch. All of that said, it is essential to note that the field of Ufology really isn't any further along now than it was sixty years ago. Scientific proof is sought after by some. Many rely incorrectly on their acceptance of the phenomenon as the evidence to prove it.

I will be the first to classify myself as a skeptic that wants to believe. Meaning, I need to see the definitive proof with no questions about what it could or could not be. Pictures and videos go a long way, but I can't test or question these. If somehow, I came across a piece of an alien spacecraft and I could test the metal, I would accept that as proof. Maybe if I sat down to a nice dinner with a little green man from Mars, I would take that as proof. Everything else is just belief or, as some believers have said to me, faith.

At this point, you are probably wondering who the hell is this guy, and why is he writing this book. Wasn't this supposed to be a book on alien encounters? Indeed, you're right, and this is a book on encounters. However, I want to set the stage first on who I am and hopefully illustrate why I ask certain questions in the interviews over the following pages. My life has been spent studying the unknown and trying to understand the deepest, darkest secrets about it. I have done this as a personal investigator, a paranormal team member, a field investigator with the Mutual UFO Network (MUFON), and most recently, a State Director for MUFON. I am a well-educated Marine, a senior leader at a well-known technology company, and a member of the Scientific Coalition of UAP Studies. I assure you I'm not prone to conspiracies and have neither had a mental disorder nor ever been institutionalized. To put it plainly, I'm a student of the unknown on a quest to educate and help those faced with the challenge of explaining the unusual things they believe they have encountered.

Over the years, I have conducted well over one hundred interviews with witnesses having extraterrestrial encounter experiences going back sixty years or more. I've listened to and questioned each person with compassion, openness, and respect. It didn't matter whether I believed or not; they certainly did. I strived to remain objective and not feed their ego or encourage them to embellish. I have purposely withheld my feelings, thoughts, and emotions related to each case. The conversations on the following pages are from my materials and notes only. No third parties or recordings were used.

Even though I have changed the reporter's names, specific dates, and locations in each story to protect their identity, I have not altered their words. The passion and raw emotion they conveyed in these interviews were like nothing I could describe. The individuals I talked to were Doctors, Nurses, Lawyers, Police Officers, Business Owners, and other very reputable and credible people. They had no reason to fabricate a story or go out of their way to talk to me. Most were afraid of being thought crazy and the majority were concerned that their friends and families would find out we talked. Each witness believed with every fiber of their being in what they said. At the end of each interview, the relief they had from just having someone to talk with that wouldn't judge them was palpable.

Whether you believe it or not is entirely up to you. As you read these sixteen different interviews, you may laugh, cry, and/or drag your hand down your face in incredulous shock. You may also think the reporters should seek immediate help from a medical professional or even quickly justify their report as something of this planet. Still, I caution you to hold back until the end. Keep your mind open. These people genuinely believe and are passionate about sharing their stories.

I ask you this: what would you do if I were interviewing you in a similar situation? Would you be brave enough to talk in the face of possible ridicule? Would you have the courage to share your experience? Ultimately, that would be your decision as it was theirs. All I ask is for you to read the interviews with an open mind and try to put yourself in their shoes. These are real people with real trauma. They are forgotten and excluded for the sheer unbelievability of their events. This book is not designed to convince you aliens are real. At its core, this is a book about the power of belief more than Alien encounters. Perhaps the interviewee's faith will educate you on both.

ENCOUNTER ONE

The Little Astronaut

INTERVIEWER: B.H. Daffern, represented as BD.
SUBJECT DETAILS:

- NAME: Gerald (alias)
- AGE AT TIME OF INTERVIEW: 70 years old
- ENCOUNTER DATE: SUMMER 1964
- OCCUPATION: Aviator (Military and Civilian) (Retired)

NOTES:

- Introductions, identity validation, platitudes, and closing statements have been removed to protect subjects identity and personal information. This may cause you to doubt the interview because of the abrupt start and end. It is by design.
- Prior to the interview, the subject was asked to submit a written account of their experience to allow preliminary investigation of their claims.
- Fillers (um, uh, basically, you know, etc.), false starts (incomplete sentences), repetitions (repeated words and sentences), and contradictions have been included.

BD: Thank you for taking the time to talk with me. I've read through your account and would love for you to tell me about

it without looking at your report. Please make sure to include any emotions, feelings, or senses. Things you might have smelled, heard, or felt. Stuff like that.

GERALD: I'll try. But before I get started, you're going to think I'm crazy. And I don't care if you don't believe me. I know it happened.

BD: Gerald, you're not crazy for believing something. I'm here to listen and see if I can help you, even if that is only documenting the experience. I'm not here to judge your level of sanity. Please don't worry about what I think or anything else.

GERALD: Ok, but you won't believe it. It was the middle of the 60's. 1964, I think. I was 16. We went to the Florida beach for my birthday. My parents rented a house along the water and we had lots of family members there. It was so noisy, I decided to go for a walk along the beach. There was no one out there. I was walking along with my feet in the water when I saw it.

BD: Saw what?

GERALD: The tiny astronaut.

BD: Then what happened.

GERALD: I ran up and grabbed it. It was really light weight, like it was hollow.

BD: What were you feeling?

GERALD: I was excited. It wasn't no doll.

BD: I didn't say it was.

GERALD: It was a shrunk astronaut. One of ours.

BD: That seems like a bit of a leap. Why don't we go back to what you had in your hands? You said it was one of ours? What do you mean by that? Can you describe it to me?

GERALD: It was about a foot long, dressed in a silver space suit, and had on a space helmet with its visor down. It had a little USA patch on its uniform. It was light.

BD: You mentioned that. What did you do next?

GERALD: What do you think I did? I took off his helmet. He was alive and needed help. He wasn't moving and seemed almost plastic. His hair looked painted on. I remember thinking its hair was blonde like mine and he had a little scar on his cheek. He didn't really have an expression, but I knew his last minutes were filled with fear.

BD: And how did you know that?

GERALD: I could feel it. I don't know how, but it was communicating with me. That's how I knew what happened to him. It was like ESP, I guess.

BD: And what had happened to him?

GERALD: He was a United States astronaut that was captured by the aliens and they shrunk him to a doll size. He had escaped and came to shore for help.

BD: At this point are you still excited? Or are you feeling anything different?

Gerald does not answer for close to twenty seconds.

BD: Gerald? Are you okay?

GERALD: (breathing heavy) I remember like it was last week.

BD: Remember what?

GERALD: I was getting scared. I knew they saw me. They were watching me.

BD: Who?

GERALD: The ones that did that to him. I had to get rid of him or they might do it to me. I stood there frozen. I couldn't move. In the distance, I heard my mom call my name. I still stood there. She then yelled something like, don't make me come get you. I was suddenly able to move and think. I threw the little man in the water and ran back towards the rented house.

BD: You said earlier you thought he was alive and needed help. Why would you throw him into the water and run away?

GERALD: If I tried to help him or stay there, I felt that I would be next. They shrink people all the time and turn them into those.

BD: Into what?

GERALD: Dolls.

BD: So, you acknowledge that it was doll like?

GERALD: Not like any doll I ever saw. My sister had dolls and they didn't look like this, plus hers had hair, not plastic paint. But it was the size of a doll.

BD: Would it surprise you to know I did some research before our talk and found something out.

GERALD: Like what?

BD: In 1964, they came out with a G.I. Joe doll that matches your description exactly and even had the scar on the cheek. It was dressed all in sliver and had a helmet. It was blonde and the hair was painted on.

GERALD: (yelling) This was no doll!

BD: I'm sorry to upset you. I was merely mentioning what I found. Is it not possible what you saw was just a toy that you had never seen before? Maybe your younger self was mistaken, or your imagination ran away on you?

GERALD: Absolutely not.

BD: Understood. Are there any other normal possibilities you considered?

GERALD: You're just like Martha.

BD: Martha?

GERALD: My dead wife.

BD: I'm sorry for your loss.

GERALD: It ain't important. She never believed me. I'm telling you it was no doll.

BD: Fair enough. Let's get back to the night of the discovery.

GERALD: It wasn't a doll.

BD: Understood. Back to the night. After you ran back to the house, what happened? Did you tell your parents or family?

GERALD: When I got back, I was still really scared from being watched. I kept tasting salt in my mouth, and I think it was a sign they were still watching. I didn't tell no one about it. I hung out with them for another hour and went to bed.

BD: About what time was it?

GERALD: Close to midnight. Oh, that was another thing. The time was different.

BD: What do you mean?

GERALD: I had gone for the walk about eight and I couldn't have gone any longer than thirty minutes, but when I got back it was almost eleven. I lost a few hours. Does that mean anything to you?

BD: It could. How familiar are you with the UFO and Extraterrestrial phenomenon?

GERALD: Not at all. That night scared me too much. I didn't want to learn nothing about no one that could do that.

BD: There are other reports of missing time.

GERALD: Ok, so you know I ain't lying about that.

BD: I haven't said I thought you were lying about anything. Missing time is often associated with alien encounters. There are several explanations. I just wanted to point it out. Please continue.

GERALD: I went to bed that night and holy cow; the nightmares were bad.

BD: What kind of nightmares, if you can remember?

GERALD: I may be seventy, but I have a good memory and that night has stayed fresh all these years. I dreamt of that little astronaut. He was in the water, barely staying afloat, and trying to swim back to shore. There was this large silver cigar hovering over him. He's screaming as it finally catches him in some beam of light and pulls him up to the ship. I can hear the aliens in the ship laughing.

BD: Did you ever see, hear, or feel anything else after that day? Any more nightmares?

GERALD: No. When I woke up the salt taste was gone from my mouth and so was everything else, I was thinking.

BD: I'm glad you mentioned that again. You were at the ocean, any chance the salt taste could have been from the water or if you had some on your hand and accidentally got it in your mouth?

GERALD: I knew you wouldn't believe me. This is a waste of time. You think I'm crazy.

BD: Not at all. I think you believe what you encountered. I wasn't there. Hell, I wasn't even born. So, who am I to tell you what you saw was real or fake. I'm on your side and just trying to make sure I get the facts right and remove any lingering doubt.

GERALD: Okay. Sorry, I got upset. I just know damn well what I experienced. And I ain't no liar or cheat.

BD: Understandable given the situation. Did you ever smell something unusual?

GERALD: No.

BD: I know you didn't tell anyone that night, but did you ever tell anyone?

GERALD: Only my wife.

BD: Did she believe you?

GERALD: (chokes up) No.

BD: And why is that?

GERALD: Why what? Why didn't I tell others or why didn't she believe me?

BD: ...Both.

GERALD: Are you daft? Would you tell people that story? I know my family and friends wouldn't believe me and I sure as hell not going to tell anyone in the military or the airlines. I'm retired now and my reputation don't matter, but it sure as hell did then. I just pushed it deep down. I never forgot a single detail.

BD: So then, why now? Why come forward?

GERALD: (sniffles and crying) It was time.

BD: What made it time?

GERALD: Excuse me.

Gerald blows his nose.

GERALD: Martha. She died three months ago. And I turned 70 the day after. I don't have many years left and with her gone, I thought it was about time someone else knew. Whether she believed me or not, she at least knew the story. She could carry it on for that little astronaut. Someone has to know his story, or he died for nothing. People have to know what these things are doing.

Every time someone disappears. You see it on the news all the time. I bet they have been shrunk and taken by these things.

BD: And what do you think these "things" are?

GERALD: Hell, if I know. But I do know that they are here to hurt us. You don't help no one from the shadows. If they were good, they wouldn't be hiding. Would they?

BD: You make a good point. Why do you think they are doing this to the human race then? Why shrink us?

GERALD: Easier to stow us. They just keep us all in a crate instead of an entire ship. You know, economy of scale.

BD: I don't think that means what you think it does, but I get your point. I know it's a sensitive subject, but why don't you think your wife believed you.

GERALD: (laughing) She was a bitch. Just kidding. She was a very loving woman, and I was lucky to have her for almost forty years. However, she was a science teacher and unless she could prove it, she wouldn't believe it. Except when it came to church. We were there every Sunday. I tried like hell to convince her of the encounter, but she would always say she knew I believed it. She just wouldn't believe in me, but she believed in God. I was all alone in knowing this.

BD: It must have been hard to carry this burden by yourself.

GERALD: You don't know the half of it. I just don't understand why she wouldn't believe me. She could have lied and said she did, but that just wasn't her. I told her that there were aliens all through the bible. Did you know that? They were there when Jesus was born.

BD: I am aware of the belief that people have of that. Some think the North Star that led the wise men to Jesus was actually a spacecraft or the bible speaks of extraterrestrials, but calls them angels and demons. It is an interesting theory.

GERALD: Yeah...yeah it is. But she wouldn't listen. Doesn't matter though. She knows the truth now.

BD: Just a few more things. More curious than anything. Do you have difficulty falling asleep or staying asleep?

GERALD: No more than anyone else.

BD: I know this might be a bit sensitive, but it helps to know. Are you taking any prescription medicine that may cause hallucinations?

GERALD: Absolutely not.

BD: Do you drink or maybe use medical marijuana? I ask only because we use it to track to see how it correlates with encounters.

GERALD: I haven't had a whiskey in ten years and I never touch the wacky tobacky.

BD: Is there anything else you would like to tell me about the encounter or anything else before or after?

Gerald goes almost thirty seconds before responding.

GERALD: Not off the top of my head. I do want to thank you for listening. This is a huge thing to have bouncing in my head for so long. Letting it out and not having you judge me has done this old man good.

Gerald sniffles followed by blowing his nose.

GERALD: I haven't been this emotional since that day except for when Martha passed. I know you can't do much with this and people will think I'm nuts. I got no proof and nothing beyond my word. But as God is my witness, I ain't lying.

BD: You're welcome and I am glad we had this time to chat.

NOTES:

After this interview, I followed up with Gerald twice to see how he was doing. He refused to talk to me and later sent me an email with the following statement, "It wasn't a doll!"

It is important to note that in my thirty plus years of interest in the field of ufology and extraterrestrial encounters, I have never heard of aliens shrinking humans. This was indeed a unique report.

ENCOUNTER TWO

National Security

INTERVIEWER: B.H. Daffern, represented as BD in transcript.
SUBJECT DETAILS:

- NAME: Nicole (alias)
- AGE AT TIME OF INTERVIEW: 38 years old
- ENCOUNTER DATE: Multiple dates. Encounters continue.
- OCCUPATION: Retail store clerk, former Air Force Airman First Class

NOTES:

- Introductions, identity validation, platitudes, and closing statements have been removed to protect subjects identity and personal information. This may cause you to doubt the interview because of the abrupt start and end. It is by design.
- Prior to the interview, the subject was asked to submit a written account of their experience to allow preliminary investigation of their claims.
- Fillers (um, uh, basically, you know, etc.), false starts (incomplete sentences), repetitions (repeated words and sentences), and contradictions have been included.

BD: Thank you for taking the time to...

NICOLE: Can I talk about it now?

BD: Sure, Nicole. Go ahead.

NICOLE: Time is of the essence. We have to stop them before they go any deeper. The government doesn't care, the police don't, and well the church...you know.... I ain't a young boy so they have no interest in me.

BD: I would like to stop you there please. I want to stick to the details of the encounter first and then we can talk about...

NICOLE: The details are we is fucked. Why doesn't anyone care?

BD: I assure you I care. So, please let's go back to the encounter. Without looking at your submittal can you please describe it to me using your senses and feelings. Things like smells and tastes. Make sense?

NICOLE: I guess, but you're wasting time.

BD: Indulge me, please.

NICOLE: The first time I saw them was when I was a kid, but I don't remember much about them other than they would just take me. They would do things to me and then put me back. I thought they were here to help.

BD: What kind of help?

NICOLE: I don't know, cure disease, get rid of retarded births, get us a better president. Just help.

BD: Do you remember anything else about that time?

NICOLE: No, not really. It isn't important. It's what happened two years ago.

BD: Did you see anything between you being a little girl to two years ago?

NICOLE: All the time.

BD: Did you ever talk to other experiencers?

NICOLE: Why?

BD: They have support groups. I know of a few good ones I could recommend if you would like to maybe attend one of them. Just let me know.

NICOLE: Can I tell my story now?

BD: I apologize.

NICOLE: I just have to get this out. So just shut up. (silence) Sorry.

BD: No worries, continue.

NICOLE: Two years ago, I was in downtown Atlanta. Just finished watching a concert, Luke Bryan or was it Jason Aldean, no maybe it was Tim McGraw, it doesn't matter. I was, no wait it was Luke Bryan. Anyway, I was walking through that park, Centennial or whatever they call it when I saw a light in the sky.

BD: Describe the light.

NICOLE: The thing was bright white, roundish, and I could tell it had writing on the bottom of it, but it was too far away. I couldn't hear anything, so I know it wasn't one of ours.

BD: How did you feel?

NICOLE: Feel?

BD: Yes. Were you scared, excited, not impacted? And did you smell anything or any other sense like stuff.

NICOLE: I guess I was excited, but I didn't smell or feel anything else. The park was crowded with people. I tapped my friend and asked if they could see it. She said what and when we both looked up it was gone. And I didn't see it again.

BD: Had you been drinking or trying anything else?

NICOLE: Of course, I was drinking. Didn't impact my eyesight.

BD: Do you wear glasses?

NICOLE: No! And I hear fine too before you ask.

BD: Was there anything else?

Nicole doesn't answer for almost thirty seconds.

NICOLE: That night nothing.

BD: Did you have your phone with you?

NICOLE: Of course. Always. And no!!!! I didn't take a picture. (agitated) I don't know why, but I didn't. I am so mad at myself.

BD: That's very common. Anything else?

NICOLE: No. But the next night, I'm in my driveway smoking a cigarette, my parents went to bed and my kid was watching TV. I looked up and I saw the same light again. It was closer this time.

BD: What time was it?

NICOLE: After ten cause that's when my parents go to be. But I remembered my phone this time, but it was inside. I thought about going in and getting it, but I was afraid it would be gone. So, I yelled to my daughter to get it. I waited a few minutes, and she didn't come. I yelled again and she still didn't come. I was pissed. I stood there and just stared at it. That fucker didn't move.

BD: Same question, what were you feeling or maybe sensing? Could you tell if anyone else around you could see it?

NICOLE: It was after ten at night, who the hell would be out there?

BD: You never know.

NICOLE: No, no one was out. As far as feeling, I was angry and scared. I was shifting from one foot to the other, half expecting it to come down and take me. But it didn't. It just hung up there.

BD: How long was it there?

NICOLE: Well, let me tell ya. After a while, I decided to go get my phone. I ran into the house, grabbed it off the counter and rushed outside. I yelled at my daughter to follow and when we got outside it was gone.

BD: About how long do you think you were looking at it before that?

NICOLE: I don't know.

BD: Did anything else happen that night?

NICOLE: Other than screaming at my daughter for ignoring me, no. She claimed she didn't hear me, but you know teenagers.

BD: Had you been drinking that night?

NICOLE: Yes! But I ain't no alcoholic. I smoke a joint occasionally, but I wasn't that night.

BD: I didn't think you were. I remember reading there was another encounter.

NICOLE: Happens all the damn time. The next one was the one that I learned the truth about them.

BD: About them?

NICOLE: The aliens. Pay attention.

BD: Sorry. I just wanted to make sure I knew what you were referring.

NICOLE: They told me they are here to take our water and impregnate us.

BD: Tell me more about that.

NICOLE: It was in the morning, a little past four. And no, I wasn't drinking or smoking. I was opening at work and had to be there at four thirty.

BD: Was it still dark?

NICOLE: It was and freezing. You may not know this, but at Wal-Mart they leave the parking lot lights on all night. I had just pulled up under one that way I can sees my way in.

BD: Seems like a good idea.

NICOLE: I locked my car and was heading in when there was a bright light above me. It was brighter than the parking lot light and seemed to be higher. I looked up and saw that same damn shape as in the park. Except this time, it was lowering. I was getting warm and started to sweat. I stopped walking.

BD: Was it voluntary that you stopped?

NICOLE: No. I couldn't move and just kept looking up. I felt like I was melting. Then a laser beam or something shot down and hit me between the eyes. All of a sudden, I knew their whole plans. They were here from a parallel world and wanted water and women. They used to be like us. They was human, but deformed. They had asked for our help, but they were turned down.

BD: Did they say who they asked?

NICOLE: They didn't say it, but I bet it was the damn democrats. But because we wouldn't work with them anymore, they decided to take what they wanted. They was going to keep taking and we couldn't stop them. (crying) They said my little girl was part their baby and that they killed her daddy because he wasn't the father and would just be in the way.

BD: That's horrible. What happened next?

NICOLE: Then I could talk.

BD: What did you say?

NICOLE: I asked how their day was. What the hell do you think I said? I told them to stop what they were doing, and they said no. I told them that my daughter wasn't half alien.

BD: What were they doing next? How were they responding to what you said?

NICOLE: (yelling) Fucking listen. They were beaming stuff in my head. Bad stuff. They showed me stuff they did to people and how their bases were under the water. And even what they looked like. Scary shit. Long necks, brown burnt skin, no lips and large head. It was all cause some radiation or fallout. Something like that. I remember breathing so heavy that I thought my heart was going to bust out my chest. They kept telling me to calm down, that I couldn't stop nothing, and if I didn't have power, then there was no reason to fight them. I told them to fuck off. That must have been what did it.

BD: Did what?

NICOLE: They let me go. I was back in the parking lot, under the same light except now the sun was up and there were lots of cars in the parking lot. I was confused and just looked around.

BD: Do you remember what time it was?

NICOLE: Oh yeah. I went into work. I had to clock in, and it was 10:13. I told my boss what happened, but he still wrote me up for being late and told me to stop lying to him. I guess if I was him, I wouldn't believe I was late because aliens abducted me. But it was the damn truth!

BD: What did you do next?

NICOLE: I just shut up and worked my shift. I need the job or I'm never getting out of my parents' house.

BD: I have a lot of questions.

NICOLE: No shit Sherlock. Ask?

BD: Have I offended you? You seem really upset at me.

NICOLE: I just hate being questioned. Go ahead.

BD: You mentioned it was the same kind of thing you saw before, and it was lowering to you. In a past encounter, you said there was writing on the bottom, but it was too far to read. Did you see writing this time and if so, could you make it out?

NICOLE: Uh...uh... I didn't think about that. Hold on. Now that I think about, I don't. It either wasn't there, or I don't remember.

BD: When you were frozen and couldn't move, what did your body feel like?

NICOLE: Feel like?

BD: Was it numb or were you in pain? Anything you can remember?

NICOLE: I guess it was tingly. Like when your foot goes to sleep. Like jelly, but pin pricks.

BD: When it let you go; did you still feel any of that?

NICOLE: Why is that important?

BD: Just curious. Sometimes, if you take a medicine regularly it can cause that tingling sensation which would be a normal explanation for the feeling, and I was trying to figure out if that was part of the incident or happens regularly.

NICOLE: I don't normally walk around tingly. I only take one medicine and it never made me feel that way before. I'm not a meth head or nothing. And again, I am not an alcoholic. I'm just trying to do right by my daughter.

BD: And which medicine would that be?

NICOLE: Seroquel, why?

BD: Isn't that used to treat schizophrenia?

NICOLE: This has nothing to do with that. I take my medicine.

BD: Ok. No worries. So, did the feeling in your legs persist?

NICOLE: No. I guess not. I was back to normal

BD: Great. Next question and I don't mean any offense by this, but why you? Why would they share with you their secret plan?

NICOLE: I guess it was cause maybe they wanted me to know about my girl. (heavy sigh) I don't know, maybe I was a good lay and it was pillow talk. They told me okay. I don't care if you don't believe me.

BD: I didn't say that. I am just trying to figure out what makes you special.

NICOLE: You mean because I live at my parents' house with my teenage daughter and work at Wal-Mart.

BD: No ma'am. Nothing like that. I just don't know why you over someone else. I bet Wal-Mart is a great job.

NICOLE: They have a good 401k.

BD: We kind of went off the track here. Please, please, please understand I am not judging you. Just trying to understand.

NICOLE: Ok. Listen, I'm just wound up over this. Everyone is calling me crazy and it just hurts. (coughs) To not be believed.

BD: I can imagine. Can I ask a few more questions?

NICOLE: Sure.

BD: Can you remember any smells, sounds, or things you saw while in their control?

NICOLE: It is all a blur. I don't remember smelling anything which is odd because the Wal-Mart parking lot usually smells like piss. I know I didn't hear anything, and it was just the bright light. It was like the sun, but didn't hurt my eyes.

BD: Did they give you any indication how long they've been here. I know you mentioned they had been working with the government, but not anymore.

NICOLE: They didn't really say. My guess is a long time because of my mom.

BD: Your mom?

NICOLE: She said that when she was a kid she was abducted too. And she is old.

BD: (laugh) Got it. So, a while. Earlier you mentioned you didn't know who said no to them. Did they say, who stopped working with them?

NICOLE: I'm sure it was Obama. They said it was the government. They had been hunting for their underwater bases and started to attack the aliens. They were peaceful until then. They only took people with government permission.

BD: I want to make sure I hear what you said correctly. The government knew people were being abducted and they let it happen?

NICOLE: Of course. That's why we have all these cool technologies. We get to reverse engineer their stuff. And they get to work on our people.

BD: That's a scary thought.

NICOLE: That's what I have been telling you. They know and when the government understood that they weren't getting a good deal, they stopped and started some secret war with the aliens. But it isn't working out. We picked a fight with someone bigger and better than us. We have to do something more or millions of Americans will die.

BD: What about the rest of the world?

NICOLE: I only care about America, but I bet the rest of the world would have problems.

BD: I bet. Something else you said, I want to dig into. Your husband? I'm sorry to hear he died.

NICOLE: He wasn't my husband, but I loved him. He was my little girl's daddy no matter what they say.

BD: How did he die?

NICOLE: The aliens killed him.

BD: Right. You mentioned that. Let me rephrase the question. How did they cover up killing him?

NICOLE: They crashed his motorcycle into the center divider on I285. They made him lose control and sent him headfirst into the wall. Then they put alcohol in his system to hide it and made everyone think he was drunk. But they was stupid, because he never drank on a work night.

BD: I'm sorry to hear this. How long ago was this?

NICOLE: Six years ago. (crying) He was a beautiful man. He never hit me with an open fist. He loved us.

BD: I'm sure he did. Thank you for sharing this. It sounds very traumatic and you are very brave to come forward.

NICOLE: That's not all. The ship is still following me.

BD: How often?

NICOLE: Every day. You could come out tonight and look up and it will be there.

BD: You mentioned though that no one else had seen it and when you do try to get someone, it disappears. Has that changed yet?

NICOLE: You would have to hide so they don't know you're around. But you could see it.

BD: You mentioned that they were here to take the Earth's women and water.

NICOLE: Yes.

BD: Why didn't they take you when they had you? You said they claim to have impregnated you. Does that mean they took you once and then released you?

NICOLE: I don't know. The next time I talk to them I'll ask them. Maybe it's only when I drink.

BD: Drink? What do you mean by that?

NICOLE: When I drink alcohol, I tend to see them more, but they don't take me. I don't know. I don't want to talk about that anymore. Any other questions?

BD: Have you taken pictures?

NICOLE: Of course. Those were the ones I attached to my last email.

BD: I opened those. They were just pictures of the night sky. There were no bright lights.

NICOLE: There was. They must have deleted it when they saw me sending them. I didn't think they were monitoring my email. They could be listening to this call. Oh shit.

BD: Let's pause for a moment. I'm curious, how much do you know about the lore of extraterrestrial life and unidentified flying objects?

NICOLE: What do you mean?

BD: Sorry. Have you read books on encounters or space craft? Watched anything on television? Stuff like that.

NICOLE: I read and watch everything I can get my hands on. The more I know about them the harder it will be for them to take me over.

BD: Understood. Just wanted to know how in-depth your knowledge was. Thank you. Sorry for the interruption.

NICOLE: Sorry? Sorry! They are still moving forward with their plans. We have to stop them. You are the last person that can help. Everyone else has pushed me away.

BD: Everyone else? Who have you told?

NICOLE: I started with my family. When they didn't listen, I went to my pastor. When he didn't listen, I went to the police, both local and state. They still pushed me away and I have started calling the military bases around the country trying to get anyone that can listen. They are taking people and going to kill us, and no one will help. It's a national emergency. I even reached out to the damn FBI.

BD: I would love to help. However, I'm not sure what I can do that those organizations couldn't.

NICOLE: So, you aren't going to help me either? We have to fight them. They have taken so much from me and done too much to me. I won't stay quiet. That is how they get us when we act like sheep. What would you do?

BD: I think the first step that might help is to connect you with a few experiencer groups. You can talk with people who may have had some of the same experiences and maybe through that you can get some support.

NICOLE: This is ridiculous. You've wasted my time. Can you at least tell me if you know of others that have had similar experiences?

BD: Not specifically. There are several documented cases with some similarities. About five percent of all abductees mention something about psychic communication or download. There are many abduction cases out there and some have found it to be a positive experience and others, like you, have horrific experiences leaving you with more questions than answers.

NICOLE: That's wonderful. We can just sit around and talk. You can email me whatever you want, but I am going to take action. You haven't heard the last from me.

The phone line disconnects.

NOTES:

After this interview, I sent Nicole the information for the experiencer group. As of this writing, she had not attended a single meeting. I emailed her twice and never heard back. I tried to call her, but her line was disconnected. Certain cases, like this one, you can only hope they have not hurt themselves.

You don't have to believe in conspiracies to wonder why so many reports of aliens and space craft have not been considered a threat to National security. The United States government neither encourages nor discourages the reporting of these events. Further, they don't seem to exhibit any interest in investigating or providing answers to the public. It makes you wonder if they know something we don't or if it is an act of denial because of past bias towards the sanity of those that see these events or have these encounters.

ENCOUNTER THREE

Making Babies

INTERVIEWER: B.H. Daffern, represented as BD in transcript.
SUBJECT DETAILS:

- NAME: Valerie (alias)
- AGE AT TIME OF INTERVIEW: 43 years old
- ENCOUNTER DATE: January 2001
- OCCUPATION: Lawyer

NOTES:

- Introductions, identity validation, platitudes, and closing statements have been removed to protect subjects identity and personal information. This may cause you to doubt the interview because of the abrupt start and end. It is by design.
- Prior to the interview, the subject was asked to submit a written account of their experience to allow preliminary investigation of their claims.
- Fillers (um, uh, basically, you know, etc.), false starts (incomplete sentences), repetitions (repeated words and sentences), and contradictions have been included.

BD: Thank you for taking the time to talk with me. I've read through your account and would love for you to tell me about

it without looking at your report. Please make sure to include any emotions, feelings, or senses. Things you might have smelled, heard, or felt. Stuff like that.

VALERIE: You are most welcome. However, before we get started, I just want to make sure once again, that my name will not be shared with anyone.

BD: Absolutely. I guarantee it. If I ever use this interview for anything, I will make sure that your identity is withheld.

VALERIE: Thank you. The DA office would not appreciate it.

BD: Understood. So, let's get started. I have read your statement and without you looking at it, can you please share with me what happened in your own words. Please make sure you share every single detail. I'm interested in what you were thinking, feelings, any senses. Don't leave a detail out.

VALERIE: This happened back in early 2001 and went on for about 6 months.

BD: I did notice the date from the report. Had anything every happened before this incident?

VALERIE: No this was the first time anything like this happened to me.

BD: Out of curiosity, why did you choose to come forward now almost twenty years later.

VALERIE: I was watching one of those shows on National Geographic, Alien Encounters or something like that. I saw a story that reminded me of mine, and it all seemed to all flood in. I felt compelled to tell someone. I do understand that you may not believe me and won't be able to do anything to help me.

BD: Have you read up on the subject or watched much on TV?

VALERIE: Not really. If it's on in the background, I might. But I don't seek it out if that's what you mean. I just felt the need to tell someone. The time was right.

BD: I hear that quite often. Sometimes we just need to be heard. Please continue your story.

VALERIE: I knew you would get it. Ok. (cough) I get a little chocked up every time I think about it. As I said, it was the beginning of 2001. I was living with my parents while in law school and it was winter break. We had this big house with high ceilings. I was sitting in the living room watching TV. It sat on a wall with very high windows. They went all the way to the A frame ceiling.

BD: Do you remember what time it was?

VALERIE: I don't, but probably close to midnight. I was watching one of those late-night shows and they were making fun of the president. It was close to a punchline when all of the lights in the house went out. It maybe lasted a few seconds, but I was instantly cold. I mean frozen to the bone. Then the lights and TV came back on and it warmed up. I remember thinking how weird this was because it was a warm night, sixty-five or seventy.

BD: Were you alone?

VALERIE: Yes. My parents were already in bed and my sister wasn't there. At this point, I didn't think much about it and settled back in. Then the TV pictures started getting wavy.

BD: What do you mean by wavy?

VALERIE: The image looked like it was shrinking and enlarging sort of like when you do a wave at the Braves game. It did this for a solid fifteen minutes. I figured the power issues were causing it. Then it went completely dark.

BD: The house lost power again?

VALERIE: No. Just the TV. It went out. Then a bright light blinded me. I held up my hand and tried to see the source of it. It was coming from the top windows by the ceiling. The light was so bright it hurt to look at, but I could definitely see it was off the ground.

BD: At this point do you hear anything, maybe smell something?

VALERIE: No, nothing. But I am starting to feel flight. You know, the fight or flight response. I have seen it in many cases where people run based on instinct. I wanted to run. I had to get away from the light.

BD: And did you?

VALERIE: No.

BD: Why not?

VALERIE: I don't know. I didn't want to leave the couch. I was afraid if I moved, they would see me.

BD: They who?

VALERIE: I don't know. But it was a they.

BD: You said the light was bright and blinded you. Were you able to see a little better after a while or did is stay blinding?

VALERIE: Oh, it was still blinding.

BD: Could it have just been a silent helicopter?

VALERIE: It didn't feel...human. I know that sounds weird and unbelievable. But I know at my core that it was not human, and it wanted me for something.

BD: If you had to guess, what do you think they wanted?

VALERIE: I don't know.

BD: Just guess for me. Take a deep breath and say the first thing that comes to your mind.

VALERIE: (breath) My body.

BD: Your body? Can you explain more?

VALERIE: They wanted to examine me or something. But I wasn't going to move. I held tight to the couch; they weren't going to get me this time. (screaming) No way in hell.

BD: Valerie, are you okay?

VALERIE: Huh?

BD: Are you okay? Seems like it got very vivid.

VALERIE: (deep breath) It was. Sorry.

BD: No worries. But you said something. You said, again. What do you mean, again?

VALERIE: Uh... Now that I think about it, this wasn't the first time. I feel like this had happened before. That's weird, I didn't remember that before. I guess it has happened before. Why can't I remember?

BD: It happens sometimes. Let's go back to this incident. What are you feeling at this point? What happened next?

VALERIE: I am just frozen. Scared to death and defiant. I'm staring at the light and I know eyes behind the light are staring back at me. Then it was gone. The TV came back on. I still stared up at the sky. I wanted to make sure they were gone.

BD: And did they come back?

VALERIE: Not that night. When I was sure they were gone, I started watching TV again. As if nothing happened. Isn't that unusual. Shouldn't I have ran away scared or hid. Why did I watch TV?

BD: Not exactly sure. Maybe shock? Who knows? What's on TV?

VALERIE: Not sure that's relevant to the event. The whole event was only five minutes or so.

BD: Humor me. Do you remember what was on TV?

VALERIE: (after moments of silence) Reruns of I Love Lucy. That's odd.

BD: And you're sure the late-night show had just started when this happened.

VALERIE: I am. But that show is almost ninety minutes long.

BD: If it felt like five minutes, why did it last at least ninety minutes.

VALERIE: That's a damn good question. I don't know.

BD: It also happens. Just out of curiosity, have you ever read anything similar to what you experienced? OR maybe seen it on a TV show?

VALERIE: You asked that before. Not that I'm aware of.

BD: Sometimes, I ask the question differently depending on the context. Let's move on. Had you been drinking that night?

VALERIE: Absolutely not. I didn't drink or do drugs.

BD: Were you on any medicines? Some doctor prescribed medicines can do funny things.

VALERIE: No. I don't like pills.

BD: Got it. What happened next?

VALERIE: Life went on and then about two months later I started having huge stomach issues. I went to a doctor. After tests and blood work, it came back that I was pregnant.

BD: Did they give you an indication of the conception date?

VALERIE: They could get it down to about a week. It's not an exact science.

BD: What date did they give you?

VALERIE: It was that week.

BD: I realize that this is a personal question, but when was the last time you had been with anyone.

VALERIE: Never.

BD: Never? Even maybe a year before.

VALERIE: I mean never. I'm a member of the LGBQ community. I have never been with a man.

BD: Given that. Did the doctors have any explanation?

VALERIE: They weren't ready to declare immaculate conception if that's what you mean. They insisted the way birth works and started asking me questions about situations of missing time or going to bars and not remember coming home. Stuff like that.

BD: They thought you may have been drugged and raped?

VALERIE: (crying) Exactly. I told them it never happened. I was a good girl. Beyond being a lesbian, I was the perfect child. My parents eventually came around, but at that point it made me weird to them. So, you can imagine how they reacted when I came home pregnant with never having been with a man. They thought I was a freak or crazy or worse, a damn liar.

BD: I'm sorry you didn't have any support.

VALERIE: I did. Just not from them. My girlfriend, once she got past the fact, I did not cheat on her, was there for me. It was hard.

BD: Did you tell the doctors or anyone about what you saw? Did you connect it to this pregnancy?

VALERIE: Not at the time. I did tell my parents and Julie about what I saw that night, but not in connection with the pregnancy.

My father decided that I must have sat on a toilet seat in a public restroom and there was sperm on it.

BD: Uh. It doesn't exactly work that way.

VALERIE: I told him that. People typically don't look at you the same after you claim that you may have been impregnated by aliens. I didn't feel the need to correct him. Plus, I wasn't sure the two things were connected at that point.

BD: What did they think about what you saw?

VALERIE: They listened but it really didn't go anywhere. Mom said she had seen something once, but that was it.

BD: When did you connect the pregnancy to the event?

VALERIE: It was four months later. And I was due to go in and check on the baby. I had seen the doctor a few months before and everything was going fine with the birth. This would have been me at about 6 months pregnant and I thought I would be showing more. So, I went to the doctor.

BD: So, we are in the summer at this point?

VALERIE: Yes.

BD: And no other incidents or lights seen?

VALERIE: Not that I can remember. But there was one night I woke up with my night clothes inside out and I was sure I had put them on right. I wrote it off though. This was me just having the doctor make sure everything was okay. So, I went in, got in that gown and the doctor came in. He asked some questions, did some feeling around, and then, I noticed a look in his eye. I asked him what was wrong. He said nothing and wanted me to get another sonogram. I went downstairs and got one of those and had to come back two days later. That whole time I was worried that there was a problem with my baby. All the things the books were telling me to expect, weren't happening. It was the longest two days of my life.

BD: I can only imagine. You said there was a look in his eyes. What kind of look?

VALERIE: It was hard to describe. Worry, I guess. When I went back, I knew my gut had been right. There was a second doctor in the room and as straight faced as possible they told me (sniffling) they said (sniffling) that I wasn't pregnant anymore.

BD: I'm so sorry. You had lost the baby?

VALERIE: No. That at least I could understand. No. I wasn't pregnant anymore. The baby was just gone. They made up some bullshit about it could happen and absorption this or that. But my baby was gone. It was there, then, it wasn't.

BD: Could they have misdiagnosed you as pregnant?

VALERIE: They claimed that might have happened too. I saw my home test. I remember the two pink lines and I still have it. They confirmed it in the hospital. Those things don't lie. I had some pregnancy feelings for a while.

BD: There are many cases where people thought they were pregnant. Had all the feelings and everything, but weren't. It's called pseudocyesis.

VALERIE: I was pregnant. I am a well-educated woman. I have never been crazy, I don't do drugs, and only occasionally have a glass of wine. You can't convince me that both tests were wrong, and I had this pseudocyesis thing at the same time.

BD: That is probably extremely rare. Did you happen to get your medical records and have them looked at by another doctor? Maybe they made a mistake.

VALERIE: I did. The day I was supposed to pick them up, there was a fire at the hospital and the entire records room went up in flames. I'm not saying it is connected to me. I am not a conspiracy theory person. But that seemed pretty damned strange.

BD: What do you think happened?

VALERIE: I don't really know.

BD: Guess for me.

VALERIE: I think that whatever put that baby in me, took it away. Maybe I was just an incubator. I will never know.

BD: And nothing else has happened since?

VALERIE: Well, just one thing. A few years ago, my wife and I decided we wanted a baby, and I was going to carry it. However, I couldn't get pregnant. We went through tons of tests and the results were surprising to say the least. Apparently, I had a medical condition that prevents me from producing eggs. I was born with it.

BD: Oh, I'm sorry to hear that.

VALERIE: Thank you. The question is if I was born that way, how could I show pregnant on two tests. Even if I absorbed it or something else, how do you explain that? That's not possible. And if I wasn't born that way, then what happened. Just more mysteries, I will never know.

BD: That is the roughest part about these. Has anything happened to you since this incident?

VALERIE: Nothing. I just can't get over it. I need answers.

BD: I completely understand. However, I have documented our conversation and will make sure people know what happened. Is there anything else you would like to tell me before or after?

VALERIE: Not off the top of my head. I do want to thank you for listening. I feel like I have been in a huge therapy session. People like you do God's work by not judging those who have had these events. I really appreciate you.

BD: You're welcome and I am glad we had this time to chat.

NOTES:

After this interview, I followed up with Valerie on two occasions. She hasn't had any additional events or if she did, doesn't remember them. I suggested that she may want to look into hypnosis therapy for the night back in 2001 and it may also help her remember if anything else has happened. Often abductees, don't remember details and experience missing time. At the time of this writing, she hasn't pursued that avenue.

As to the subject of extraterrestrial beings breeding with humans, this is actually quite a common belief in the ufology lore and talked about a lot. There are typically two reasons why people believe this happens. The first reason is that aliens are unable to have children and the second, they want to breed with humans to take over our planet. It is important to note that there has been no proof to this even happening, let alone the reason.

Thousands of people have been interviewed and put under hypnotic regression and recall events like this report. However, to date there has been no DNA evidence to prove it. The only fact that exists is that in the United States at least one mother a year is the victim of Fetal abduction, the kidnapping of a baby from their mother's womb.

ENCOUNTER FOUR

Dinner with ET

INTERVIEWER: B.H. Daffern, represented as BD in transcript.
SUBJECT DETAILS:

- NAME: Michelle (alias)
- AGE AT TIME OF INTERVIEW: 39 years old
- ENCOUNTER DATE: January 2011
- OCCUPATION: Nurse

NOTES:

- Introductions, identity validation, platitudes, and closing statements have been removed to protect subjects identity and personal information. This may cause you to doubt the interview because of the abrupt start and end. It is by design.
- Prior to the interview, the subject was asked to submit a written account of their experience to allow preliminary investigation of their claims.
- Fillers (um, uh, basically, you know, etc.), false starts (incomplete sentences), repetitions (repeated words and sentences), and contradictions have been included.

BD: Thank you for taking the time to talk with me.
MICHELLE: You are welcome.

BD: Before we jump into it, I want to ask something up front. How much do you know about the extraterrestrial being phenomenon and unidentified flying objects?

MICHELLE: I've read a few books, saw a few shows on TV, and maybe a movie or two. I would say just general knowledge. Why?

BD: Just something I like to check in with people on. It helps drive the discussion. Anyway, on to your event. I've read through your account and would love for you to tell me about it without looking at your report. Please make sure to include any emotions, feelings, or senses. Things you might have smelled, heard, or felt. Stuff like that.

MICHELLE: It's kind of weird to talk about, but I think someone has to know and hopefully you can help me determine what it was.

BD: If I can, I will, but to set expectations up front, that is unlikely. There are very few people that come forward when it comes to talks of aliens. Which makes it hard to coordinate events. We do get quite a few UFO reports. However, those typically are lights in the sky at a distance. All I can hope for is someone was as brave as you in sharing their story. If not, I can document in case someone else comes forward. Either way, I will do my best to investigate your claims and find some type of answer or resolution. It's just rare.

MICHELLE: That sounds frustrating

BD: You have no idea.

MICHELLE: (laughs) Where would you like me to start?

BD: Please start at the time of the event and make sure to include thoughts, feelings, or even any sensations you might have had.

MICHELLE: Sure. Okay. This was back in 2011. My husband and I were driving home from a dinner with some friends. We live off the road a bit. The house is next to a farm. The road had cornfields on one side. Anyway, it was after ten sometime, maybe closer to eleven. It was a clear night, no fog. My husband was driving and suddenly he hit the brakes. My arm shot up to the dash and I dropped my phone.

BD: Were you looking at your phone or did you see why he slammed the brakes?

MICHELLE: I was looking at my phone and didn't see it, but Mike did it on purpose.

BD: What did Mike tell you?

MICHELLE: There was some four-foot tall, brown something on two legs that darted across the road and into the corn field. At first, he thought it might have been a little black boy. But he moved too quick for that.

BD: Had either of you been drinking that night?

MICHELLE: Yes. But Mike was fine to drive. I'm a nurse, I would know. I think he had like three beers. I immediately screamed at him and cursed him for making me drop my phone. Those things are expensive to fix.

BD: For sure.

MICHELLE: But then he told me what he saw. We got out of the car. He wanted to go look for it in the corn. I was like, hell no. But he insisted. He wanted to make sure whoever it was that they weren't hurt. He grabbed a flashlight from the glove compartment and headed in. I remember thinking how glad I was he turned on the hazard lights on the car cause as we went deeper, I could see how far the car was away from us.

BD: At this point what are you thinking or feeling?

MICHELLE: I am thinking I was a fucking idiot for following him in. (laughs) I have seen enough horror movies to know how this ends. It was a dumb move. But Mike wanted to make sure whatever it was wasn't hurt. At least that's what he told me at the time. Later, he told me he thought it was a tiny big foot or something. You know we see them in our neck of the woods.

BD: I was not aware.

MICHELLE: Yeah, we are up near Helen and they are over that area. I could tell you some stories. There was this one time when we heard the roar of one of them and then the dog disappeared.

BD: I'm sure that's an interesting story, but let's stay focused on the encounter.

MICHELLE: Right. So, we walked around that cornfield for about forty minutes and saw nothing. We headed back towards the car and it was just by chance he flashed the light to the ground. That's when we saw the footprint or whatever you would call it. It looked like it was made by a bowl with three Cheetos coming off one side. They were spread a little apart, like toes.

BD: Did you happened to get a picture of it?

MICHELLE: No. Sadly. Didn't think about it. Mike stared at it a minute, looked around, grabbed my hand and ran back to the car. Every time I fell back, he would give me a yank to keep up. He was spooked.

BD: Did he ever tell you what spooked him?

MICHELLE: Sort of. He felt like he was being watched and was filled with fear.

BD: How about you?

MICHELLE: I thought it was odd, but I was more scared by Mike's reaction than to anything around me. I'd never seen him scared like that before and really didn't see it again until you know, the accident.

BD: What accident?

MICHELLE: When he died.

BD: I am so sorry. I had no idea. I was going to ask to interview him next. I'm sorry for your loss.

MICHELLE: Thank you. It happened last month. I have come to grips with it. The circle of life and all.

BD: Let's move on, I'm sorry to bring up bad memories. You don't have to talk about the accident.

MICHELLE: It's fine really. The accident happened at the house. He was out working on the car. He was under it and something went wrong with the jack and fell on him. It caused a lot of internal damage in his chest. I heard him scream. It was ear piercing. I ran out to him and just saw him there. I immediately called 911 and stayed with him. The look on his face and his actions was a mixture of confusion, pain, and downright terror. That's what he looked like that night. Just maybe not the pain. When they came and lifted the car off, the pressure decreased and everything that was damaged expanded. He didn't live long after that.

BD: I'm so sorry to hear that.

MICHELLE: (sniffling) Let's talk more about the next time.

BD: Right. Okay. Before we move on, one other question. Did you smell anything unusual out in the field or feel any change in temperatures?

MICHELLE: Not that I can recall. Fields sort of always smell like manure and that just fills the nostrils.

BD: No worries, just curious. So, what happened next.

MICHELLE: We got in the car and drove back to the house. We got ready for bed without talking much. I asked him what he thought he saw, and he would shrug. I thought it was weird he wouldn't talk about it. It was really scaring me. I kept trying to talk to him, but he would only give one-word answers and vague ones at that. At one point, he said, let's talk in the morning. He was tired and wanted to sleep. We crawled into bed and he went to sleep right away. But I didn't.

BD: Do you remember about what time this was?

MICHELLE: I don't. Probably midnightish.

BD: Beyond your concern about Mike, any other thoughts, emotions, or sensations going on.

MICHELLE: Nope. But that changed later.

BD: Go on.

MICHELLE: I laid there awake and watched him sleep. It was about 3am when I heard a sound outside. Sounded like someone was digging in our trash cans. We had a problem with critters getting in our trash before and every time we did, Mike would go out, scare them away. We also had a pellet gun next to the back porch to give those bandits an incentive to stay away. Mike had said in the past to wake him if I heard them out there and he wanted to address it when it happened. But we had the rough night and all and he was asleep. So, I decided to take care of it.

BD: You mean to go out and chase the racoons or whatever was in your garage?

MICHELLE: Yes. I was annoyed, but wanted to let him sleep. I went downstairs and grabbed the pellet gun and went out the back door. The cans are around the side of the house. When I stepped outside, there was this heaviness in the air. I felt my breath getting shorter and I don't know how else to put it, heavy.

BD: Was there any odors or just a shortness of breath?

MICHELLE: Nothing I can remember. Just a struggle to catch my breath.

BD: Did you feel anything else? Like fear, excitement, stuff like that?

MICHELLE: Sort of. I felt like I needed to rush back in the house. But I figured that it had to do with Mike and not real fear I had. So, I walked around to the cans. At this point they stopped moving. A house light on the porch was the only thing shining in the area and I didn't have a flashlight. There were shadows everywhere. I moved around the cans to stand under the light to get a better view. As soon as I did this, something shot out of the cans, screeching. The suddenness of it knocked me on my butt and I screamed. My heart was racing something bad.

BD: What did you see?

MICHELLE: A little brown thing. It moved too quick to see much else.

BD: Would you say it looked like what Mike described to you earlier?

MICHELLE: Absolutely. I grabbed the gun, got to my feet and started to head back to the house, but suddenly felt fine. The air wasn't heavy, I wasn't scared. I turned back to the cans. One was on its side, the one that that thing jumped out of. I saw those same footprints that we saw in the cornfield. I was suddenly filled with strong curiosity. I traced it's path from when it rushed by me. There was a set of trees in the dark. You are going to think I'm crazy, but I started walking towards the area. I had the pellet gun raised cause I felt something there.

BD: At this point, you are still not scared?

MICHELLE: Not at all. I stopped a few feet from the trees and started talking. I talked like I do to patients. It's okay, I said. You can come out. Maybe I can help you. There was nothing but silence, but I still felt something. So, I waited a few minutes and asked if it was hurt and or hungry. More time passed and I thought I was talking to nothing and getting ready to leave. It was then it stepped out. This brown alien with a short body, weird feet, and a huge head. It was naked, but I didn't see a penis or vagina or anything like that.

BD: Did it talk to you?

MICHELLE: It's lips didn't move, but I guess it telepathically told me stuff. It said it was a friend. I dropped the weapon, and it came closer. It held out it's wrinkly arms and it's neck extended up, so his head was higher than mine. Sort of like a giraffe. On one hand, he had a finger glowing a bright red. I heard, felt, whatever, him say he was hungry. But he said it weird, like eattt a lottt. The 't' sounded like he thought it went on longer than it should.

BD: I read that part of your submission and was curious. Do you think he was digging in your garbage for food?

MICHELLE: Oh yeah, for sure. I offered to make him a sandwich if he wanted to come in. His head lowered back down, and he waddled towards me.

BD: I need to be candid with you and with all due respect, I know this story.

MICHELLE: You've heard it before?

BD: Have you ever seen the move E.T. the Extraterrestrial. It's a film by Steven Spielberg from the eighty's.

Michelle does not respond. After about thirty seconds, I continued.

BD: Michelle, are you there?

MICHELLE: Yes. I'm here.

BD: Have you ever seen the movie?

MICHELLE: I have, but it was different. I was afraid you wouldn't believe me. You think I am making this all up. Mike did too.

BD: I am not saying that. I'm just saying it is quite similar to the film.

MICHELLE: Maybe they encountered the same aliens. I don't know. Plus, the alien in that movie was brown like shit. This guy was light brown like dirt. I supposed you're going to tell me that the alien in ET liked beer too.

BD: Actually, there is a whole scene where he drinks it. I know the movie well. It was what got me interested in people from other worlds.

MICHELLE: Well, if you don't want to hear the rest, you don't have too. It was real and I made a friend. We ate, laughed, and had a few beers.

BD: I'm sorry I upset you. I just needed to point that out. Please continue. What happened after that?

MICHELLE: What do you think happened? He ate and drank and then I walked him out into the trees. He had a ship there waiting. I think they were collecting plant samples. Anyway, he told me he loved me, got on his ship, and I never saw him again. I know he is out there and watches me from the cornfield sometimes, but we never ate together again.

BD: During this whole time, you felt safe?

MICHELLE: Yes

BD: Did you ever wake your husband?

MICHELLE: No. I told him the next day though. He didn't believe me. I even took him out to the field where the ship was and there was evidence.

BD: Really? Now that's interesting. What kind of evidence?

MICHELLE: Someone had been picking flowers out there. Just like the ones I saw getting picked that night.

BD: Got it.

MICHELLE: They probably have grown back since. You wouldn't find anything. I know they are out there though. I can feel them.

BD: You mentioned your husband didn't believe you. Did he ever say more about what he saw that night?

MICHELLE: Nothing. Every time I brought it up, he would shut it down and not talk about it. He just wanted to forget what he saw and what I told him. It was like it never happened, but I know it did. I lost my job at the hospital for talking about it. I eventually started working in an old folks home. But everyone I talked to just looked at me like I was crazy and needed help. So, I shut up about it.

BD: That's just how some people deal with it. They don't want to talk, or they pretend it didn't happen. This happened in 2011, why come forward now?

MICHELLE: Mike just died and I'm not sure if they will ask me soon to go in the ship with them. We never had kids, so if they do, I would probably go with them. I just wanted someone to know.

BD: Thank you for sharing this. As I said before, if I can find some answers for you, I will definitely try. Is it alright if I ask you a few more questions of a more personal nature?

MICHELLE: Sure.

BD: Do you wear glasses?

MICHELLE: I don't.

BD: I know shadows and trees, especially in the wind, can imitate and give false since of motion. Did you look at the alien and see details on its face?

MICHELLE: Absolutely. This was no tree. It had features like eyes and a mouth, but no nose.

BD: Did you or have you ever been on prescription medicine?

MICHELLE: I have.

BD: As a nurse, I'm sure you know of the side effects. Were any of them stated to cause hallucinations.

MICHELLE: There was one and I was on it at the time. However, Mike had seen it too.

BD: Understood. But you were on them and then had beer, correct?

MICHELLE: I did. But I was fine. I would know if I wasn't.

BD: Not always, but I hear what you are saying. Why do you think they choose to befriend you or come to your property?

MICHELLE: I think about this a lot. It was probably just random. They were hungry. I'm not any kind of extraordinary person. I think it was just two ships in the night.

BD: Do you know if the corn fields had its crop harvested or not?

MICHELLE: I think so, why?

BD: Why didn't they just eat the corn?

MICHELLE: How the hell should I know. Maybe they are allergic or didn't know.

BD: But they knew about the trash cans?

MICHELLE: I have no idea; it was just what they did.

BD: Gotcha.

MICHELLE: I'm not going to hear from you again, am I? But that's okay. You can think I'm crazy, it just felt good to tell someone.

BD: I can feel that you believe it. I don't think you're crazy. It's just wild. I will let you know if I find anything.

MICHELLE: Thank you.

NOTES:

I left Michelle three voicemails after confirming two people in the area reported lights in the sky that night that they could not explain. I never did speak with Michelle again. However, I did receive an email about a year after this talk with a message from her saying that they had not come back and that she was moving to Arkansas. She thanked me again and said to contact her if anyone reported something similar. Further, she said she had passed on my information to the new homeowners and told them to contact me if they saw anything. I sent her a response email, but she never responded. In addition, I have never heard from the new homeowners. Not sure if they saw something as well.

ENCOUNTER FIVE

The Two Bob's

INTERVIEWER: B.H. Daffern, represented as BD in transcript.
SUBJECT DETAILS:

- NAME: Bobby (alias)
- AGE AT TIME OF INTERVIEW: 69 years old
- ENCOUNTER DATE: June 2019
- OCCUPATION: Retired Judge

NOTES:

- Introductions, identity validation, platitudes, and closing statements have been removed to protect subjects identity and personal information. This may cause you to doubt the interview because of the abrupt start and end. It is by design.
- Prior to the interview, the subject was asked to submit a written account of their experience to allow preliminary investigation of their claims.
- Fillers (um, uh, basically, you know, etc.), false starts (incomplete sentences), repetitions (repeated words and sentences), and contradictions have been included.

BD: Thank you for taking the time to talk with me.
BOBBY: You are most welcome Mr. Daffern.

BD: Please. Brian is fine.

BOBBY: Then you may call me Bobby.

BD: Thank you Bobby. I read through what you emailed me. Without looking at it, can you please tell me about your incident and this time use emotions, feelings, senses...anything you can think about.

BOBBY: As they say in the theater, all the feels.

BD: I thought you mentioned you were a retired Judge?

BOBBY: I am that. At 65 I retired and started dabbling in theater. I haven't been in anything major, but that's where all the cute boys are.

BD: Got it. Please continue Bobby.

BOBBY: Over the last year, I have had a nightly visitor to my bedroom. It's not every night. I have tried to chart it out like a period or something, but there is no rhyme or reason to it. He comes when he wants, I guess. (laughs)

BD: You say over the last year? Did anything happen right before this started? Any type of event or situation that may have preceded it?

BOBBY: It started about a month before my roommate Bob moved in. My previous roommate and I had a breaking up if sorts and he left. I was alone for about a month until Bob came in. That was the time it all started.

BD: And it continues until today?

BOBBY: It does. Last night to be more precise.

BD: Wow, that's pretty recent. (laugh) So, just to be clear you prefer to go by Bobby and your roommate goes by Bob? Isn't that confusing?

BOBBY: No. Why would that be? His parents named him Bob, mine is short for Robert. Two very different origins my dear.

BD: Got it. And what kind of judge were you?

BOBBY: Family court. Why?

BD: Wanted to be more precise and fill it in. Please continue.

BOBBY: Last night was no different than any of the other nights and I know you are going to want to have me committed after hearing this. I have only told Bob about it. He believes me, by the way. Since he lives here, I wanted him to be aware in case he saw, heard, or felt something. I felt I had to do it.

BD: Understood. It would be bad if he moved in and had experiences and didn't know what else was going on.

BOBBY: The only difference is Bob thinks it's a ghost and I know in my heart that it is an alien. Because of the exuberant lights I see out my window after the event. He leaves, starts up his spaceship, and flies off.

Bobby abruptly stops and is silent.

BD: Please continue.

BOBBY: Last night, I went to bed at the same time I always do. The last thing I remember is Family Guy on TBS which I know ends at eleven. I drifted off shortly after that. The next thing I know is I'm awake. I can only move my eyes. The rest of my body is stuck. I know what this is, but it still is just as scary as every other time. I lay there helpless and I see a large figure in the door. It's black so I can't see the details. He is tall because his head touches the top of the door jamb and he is wide because he has to turn sideways to come in. He stands there and stares at me. I'm staring back. I try to speak, but my mouth can't move, and nothing comes out. I notice that I am sweating profusely. But the room is cold. I can feel the coolness and the sweat. He takes a few steps closer to me and stops again. I can hear whining. It's me. I know what he's going to do. He takes a few more steps closer. I think he wanted to make sure that I was not able to move. He is standing right next to my bed. I see him there, but he is still just a black blob. I can see no features. He pulls the covers off my body. I struggle to move, but I can't. He pulls my pajama bottoms down and exposes me. Using one hand, he gets me hard and strokes me until I ejaculate. I feel so used. He then has a napkin in his hand. Not sure where it came from. He wipes me off and pulls up my pants. I still struggle to move. He says, "Thank you for the sample." Then, leaves sideways out the door. A minute or so later I hear a beep, then my window is filled with a bright light and it slowly diminishes. I close my eyes and the next thing I know; I'm waking up and it's morning. And that's what happens. I get raped continually by a big black blob randomly.

BD: That's an extraordinary tale.

BOBBY: Told you that you wouldn't believe me.

BD: I didn't say that. It isn't whether I believe it or not. It's that you believe it. That was just a lot of information and as you can imagine it sparks a lot of questions.

BOBBY: Like what?

BD: Some of these might be sensitive, but I think it is important to understand for the documentation and understanding of this event.

BOBBY: You can ask me anything. I'm an open book.

BD: With all due respect, do you drink often or maybe use drugs for recreational purposes?

BOBBY: What?

BD: Just need to eliminate it as a possible cause. It's important to be honest.

BOBBY: Fine. Yes, I do drink and have been known on occasion to get drunk. But not every night and I don't do drugs.

BD: Got it. Is there any correlation to your drinking and visits? Do they come to try and take advantage of your relaxed state?

BOBBY: Not that I can collaborate.

BD: Did you smell anything unusual in the room when the shadow person was there?

BOBBY: I didn't. Or if I did, I just don't remember. I can try to pay closer attention when it happens again.

BD: Great. Out of curiosity, do you watch TV when you go to bed?

BOBBY: I do. Why?

BD: Do you ever fall asleep with it on?

BOBBY: All the time.

BD: Thinking back to this last encounter do you recall if you fell asleep with the TV on?

BOBBY: I'm pretty sure I did.

BD: You didn't mention it during your description. Do you have a timer or something to turn it off or was it still on?

Bobby is silent.

BD: Bobby, you there?

BOBBY: I'm here. I don't know. The TV was off, so I guess I'm wrong. I must have turned it off.

BD: Do you ever have any vivid dreams or nightmares?

BOBBY: Not that I can remember. I may, but I doubt it.

BD: Have you ever been abused in your life? As a child or adult?

BOBBY: How did you know that?

BD: Just a standard question. I will take that as a yes.

BOBBY: Ok. Yes, my uncle did when I was twelve. He would repeatedly attack me.

BD: Did he ever pay for his crimes or get caught?

BOBBY: No. He died in a car wreck, so he got his.

BD: Have you ever heard of Adult Attachment Disorder?

BOBBY: No.

BD: When a child experiences abuse from a parent or close adult it can create disorders that continue on into adult life. There are a ton of them, but essentially the lack of a sense of security and protection causes you to create coping mechanisms just to survive. Some of them can come out many years later. These children learn to adapt by withholding their own emotions and making waves. Masking their fear, anger and sadness in incidents like Alien Abduction. I'm not saying this is that, but have you considered that?

BOBBY: That's ridiculous. And if I am being truthful, quite hurtful of you to say.

BD: I'm sorry. Sometimes things like this can be going on and you may not even be aware. However, I wanted to bring it up.

BOBBY: Well, it isn't that. If it was, then Bob would not have seen it as well.

BD: Your roommate has seen it?

BOBBY: I told you. He thinks it was a ghost.

BD: Do you think he would be willing to be interviewed?

BOBBY: No. He doesn't want to talk about it.

BD: Had he had similar experiences as you?

BOBBY: Yes. But no more about him.

BD: Ok. If he changes his mind, please do pass on my contact info. Back to your latest incident. I have a few more direct questions.

BOBBY: (sigh) Go ahead.

BD: Thank you. You mentioned the alien was a he. How did you know that?

BOBBY: I just felt it. The shape and build, it would have to be a guy. Also, he had big hands.

BD: Okay, but you don't know for sure.

BOBBY: Just a feeling.

BD: Do you think he may have had features, but because of not having glasses or contact in you just couldn't see it?

BOBBY: I have excellent eyesight. I would have known. He had no features. I'm not lying to you.

BD: I didn't mean to imply that, just standard questions. I have some more specifics. You said he wiped you with a napkin. Where did the napkin go?

BOBBY: (silence) I never thought of it. I don't know. I guess he took it with him.

BD: Ok. You mention that he pulls your blanket and pajamas down and when done pulls your pajamas up. What about the blanket?

BOBBY: (silence) I don't know. I haven't thought about it. Why do you keep asking these questions? I told you what happened, and it just seems that you are asking a bunch of stupid shit.

BD: I'm sorry you feel that way. I am trying to establish if it could just be a real vivid dream and looking for signs that might be different if one was asleep.

BOBBY: I was not asleep.

BD: I'm just investigating. It is not meant as a judgement. The other thing I find interesting is that you mentioned you heard a beep and saw lights through your window. What did the beep sound like?

BOBBY: Sort of like when you unlock your car.

Bobby goes silent.

BOBBY: And no! (raised voice) It was not a car. It just sounded like it. It was a spaceship.

BD: A few more questions. You mentioned sweating quite a bit. Is that normal for you or something connected when you see this being?

BOBBY: Seems to only be when I see him. On the nights he doesn't come, I don't notice any sweating.

BD: Have you ever heard of night sweats?

BOBBY: No. Is that a thing?

BD: It is definitely a thing. It's not really uncommon to sweat during the night. You know it really depends on how many blankets you have on and how warm your house is. It could even happen depending on what you ate before bed. When you say cold sweats, are your pajamas and bedding really wet or just damp?

BOBBY: Oh, it's soaked. But like I said, the room is cold.

BD: Cold sweats normally aren't too serious. In some cases, however, regular episodes of night sweating could indicate a potentially serious medical condition. They're often associated with your body's "fight or flight" response. This happens when your body prepares itself to either run away or to get hurt. They're also common to conditions that prevent oxygen or blood from circulating throughout your body.

BOBBY: My last checkup said I was fine. I don't think it is medically related.

BD: Understood. I like to share all angles. Next question. When you go to sleep, do you lock your house or maybe your bedroom door?

BOBBY: I do lock up the house, but not my bedroom. Come to think of it, I do pull the door shut at night though. So, the alien must open the door before he stares at me. I guess that makes sense.

BD: Is it possible that someone breaks in?

BOBBY: I may be willing to say yes if it was one time. But you trying to tell me someone breaks in on a regular basis, jerks me off, and then leaves without stealing anything. Come on.

BD: Just trying to see if we have thought of every angle. Have you ever heard of sleep paralysis?

BOBBY: Is that the thing where you are asleep but think you're awake?

BD: Sort of yeah. It's that time right before you fall asleep or wake up in which you might be aware, but unable to move or speak. During this you could hallucinate which often drives a deep fear or even mix in dreams with the waking world. The key here though is not being able to move which is similar to what you said.

BOBBY: Not a dream and not a hallucination.

BD: I understand. I just want to dive a little deeper into it. Do you typically get a full night of sleep? Seven or eight hours?

BOBBY: When I'm not getting jerked off.

BD: I understand your frustration. I would like to just understand a bit more before dismissing sleep paralysis.

BOBBY: If you must.

BD: Have you had a lot of stress lately?

BOBBY: No. Well, nothing more than being helpless every night.

BD: Understood. How about your sleep position? You indicated you are on your back when this happens. Is that how you sleep?

BOBBY: I do. Does it matter?

BD: It could. Have you thought about doing a sleep study just to rule out anything medical?

BOBBY: It would just be a waste of time and money. It is really happening. Bob has seen it.

BD: I understand that and hopefully someday Bob will want to talk it over. Without his statements, I only have our conversation to go on. In the meantime, I am just trying to understand if this could fit into a natural explanation. I do this only in hope of helping you find an answer.

BOBBY: (raised voice) It's not a leftover abuse affect or a dream, or an intruder, or a fucking hallucination. Aliens are abusing me, and I need help.

BD: I hear you. Curious, have you read any materials based on encounters with extraterrestrial beings?

BOBBY: Not really. I did love Science Fiction books when I was a kid. I do love ghost shows, but really haven't got into the alien or spaceship stuff.

BD: No worries. Just curious. I like to see how people think their stories might line up with others.

BOBBY: I haven't ever heard a story like mine, but again, I haven't researched it either. It's a horrific thought to think that others out there are getting abused. If I hear of one, I will be sure to call you.

BD: No worries. Just checking. Well, anyway. Next steps. If possible, I would like to visit your home, take some readings, and possible see if I can find any physical evidence to help better figure this out. Is that something you would be open to doing?

BOBBY: Yes. That would be wonderful. I have a spare room and you could stay the night. Maybe two nights.

BD: Well, I would like to just survey the area first and then we can go from there. When would be a good time?

BOBBY: Anytime...wait...hold on? (shuffling papers and some keyboard clicking)

BD: Sure, no problem

BOBBY: It will have to be next month. Next week is my cataract surgery. But after that things look good.

BD: I need to ask one more thing. Just to be clear for my records. You mentioned you had excellent vision earlier?

BOBBY: Yes.

BD: Cataract surgery is usually because the lens of your eye has become cloudy and it makes it more difficult to read, drive, see people especially in the dark.

BOBBY: Not me. It's just cloudy. Doesn't impact my vision at all. Now do you want to come or not?

BD: Sure.

BOBBY: I will call you next month after my surgery and we will set up a time. Thank you.

Bobby hangs up the phone.

NOTES:

Bobby didn't call the following month or the month after that. I called him back in the third month and it was answered by a younger sounding man who identified himself at Bob. This Bob said that the older Bobby had changed his mind about me coming out and has nothing more to say. The younger sounding Bob did sound similar to the older sounding Bobby I had spoken with. I asked if this was the Bob I talked to or the roommate and the line immediately went dead. It seemed possible they could have been the same person. To date, I have never heard back.

Bobby was not open to this event or events being a case of hypnopompic or sleep paralysis with hallucinations. It is reported that up to four out of ten people may experience this terrifying event in their lives at least once with some having a chronic issue with it. Studies have shown it to be a discordance between the cognitive/perceptual and motor aspects of rapid eye movement (REM) sleep. Awakening sleepers become aware of an inability to move, and sometimes experience intrusion of dream mentation into waking consciousness such as seeing intruders in their bedroom.

ENCOUNTER SIX

Psychic Medium to the Stars

INTERVIEWER: B.H. Daffern, represented as BD in transcript.
SUBJECT DETAILS:

- NAME: Aaron (alias)
- AGE AT TIME OF INTERVIEW: 31 years old
- ENCOUNTER DATE: February 2020
- OCCUPATION: Psychic Medium

NOTES:

- Introductions, identity validation, platitudes, and closing statements have been removed to protect subjects identity and personal information. This may cause you to doubt the interview because of the abrupt start and end. It is by design.
- Prior to the interview, the subject was asked to submit a written account of their experience to allow preliminary investigation of their claims.
- Fillers (um, uh, basically, you know, etc.), false starts (incomplete sentences), repetitions (repeated words and sentences), and contradictions have been included.

BD: Thank you for taking the time to speak with me. I received your email and let's just say, it was one of the more unique reports I've received.

AARON: It seemed like something I should share.

BD: Thank you. If you could share your story with me and include any emotions, senses, and feelings you might have.

AARON: Sure. As I mentioned in my email, I'm a psychic medium. I'm also a spiritual coach. What that means is I can speak to the souls of the departed and connect with the souls of those still living. In other words, with permission, I can talk to the true nature of someone living of passed.

BD: I appreciate the clarification.

AARON: You're welcome. I like to make sure people understand the scope.

BD: So how does that work? If I am alive, you can connect with my soul?

AARON: Exactly. With your permission, I can interact with your true self and in some cases help you get answers to questions that might be eluding you. Sometimes the answers we seek are within us.

BD: Is it like regression therapy? We do that with some alien abduction victims or in some cases, with people who don't know what happened. So, is it like that?

AARON: Not really. You are always present during the reading. You don't ever just go to sleep.

BD: Interesting. Sorry to take us down a rabbit hole.

AARON: Completely understandable. Anyway, a week ago I was doing a reading for a regular client. And like most readings, they are only interested in future love, money, death, or difficult life choices. I wasn't connecting to any of the people she wished to talk to. I was about ready to give up, but then they seemed to jump in and wanted to speak.

BD: Who?

AARON: The aliens. Well, the Pleiadians to be specific. They gave me such a beautiful message and I wanted to make sure I shared it with the world.

BD: That's fascinating. Part of what I try to do in these types of investigations is look for proof of extraterrestrial life. Was there anything they gave you that might help me locate proof?

AARON: They came through to me, which means they do exist, so that's proof. I can't talk to the air.

BD: With all due respect, not many folks believe in psychics, so I can't really use your incident as proof that they exist. People will just say you made it up or worse that you were slightly off your rocker.

AARON: I understand. I can't help the naysayers.

BD: Curious though, were these live aliens or dead ones. You mentioned you could connect to both.

AARON: I believe they were alive. I didn't think to ask about that. They just came through and I assumed they were either in orbit or on their base off of Los Angeles.

BD: They have a base in Los Angeles?

AARON: Yes. It's under water and they have been there for many years. Listen, do you want to hear their message.

BD: Sorry, just so curious. Please go ahead.

AARON: They came through with a beautiful message. I wrote down their exact message. Their voices are rhythmic. Very soothing and jazz like. Here's what they said. Humanity has lost their way. Peace, love, and harmony is the path to ascension and should be followed to experience the true meaning of life. The time you spend in war does nothing but degrade your spirit and make you the enemy of a higher power. Trust your soul to know what is right and listen to your inner voices. Your leaders need to be taken away from their power and society, no matter what land they are on, needs to rise up and support each other. Tearing others down will not solve any of the problems. Humanity is on its third round and needs to get it right this time. And that's the message.

BD: Wow. That was beautiful. Do you happen to know what they meant by some of those messages or the intention in sharing it?

AARON: They share to help us grow and to be better. They are concerned for us and want us to love one another.

BD: How about specific to the 'humanity is on its third time around' message?

AARON: Oh yes. I'm sorry. I bet that could be confusing. There is a belief, which they are confirming, that everything we are experiencing now has happened before. Specifically, twice before. I'm not sure how many years each period lasts, but it seems the end each time is the result of us destroying ourselves, the Earth recovers, and we start again. I believe they want us to get it right this time and maybe they weren't here or involved in the other two cycles. I don't know if this is our last chance or if there is another reason. They just really want us to get this right.

BD: Have you talked with them in the past?

AARON: Sure. I talk to both the Arcturians and Pleiadians. They often have messages and talk with me. This was the first time I received such a beautiful message.

BD: And this is all in your head?

AARON: Psychically, if that's what you mean. Yes.

BD: Any idea why they chat with you as opposed to others? Is there something special about you?

AARON: I wouldn't put it that way. (laughs). The short answer is they talk to everyone who happens to be able to tune in to their frequency. To put it simply, if you call them, they will answer. It's not just me that talks with them. Many have. If you search the Internet, you probably will find a ton of references to psychic communication with them.

BD: Fascinating. I will look that up. I have heard of them, but not of the psychic communication method. Do you know what the Arcturians and Pleiadians look like?

AARON: Not really. I tend to hear them more than see them. But they are different. The Arcturians tend to be funnier than the Pleidians. They make jokes and don't sound as poetic as the Pleidians. I've received other messages that have helped me on my path to where I am today, but beyond that we just chat sometimes.

BD: Why do you think they talk with you?

AARON: Oh, it's not just me. Google them. There are many people in contact with them and having meaningful conversations and similar psychic connections. The Pleiadians are described by some that have seen them as Nordic looking and Arcturians are more reptilian like.

BD: I'm aware of both and those reports. I just haven't heard of them being so chatty with people. (laugh)

AARON: (laugh) Guess, I'm just lucky.

BD: Do they ever tell you about their plans or things they're going to do?

AARON: Not directly. I mean I never get message saying we will be in New York on Friday. It's more like this message or a conversation.

BD: Do they ever ask you questions or want you to do anything?

AARON: No. This is the first time I heard a message and felt compelled to share it.

BD: So, if this is the first time you received this kind of message, what do you normally talk about?

AARON: All kinds of things. Race issues, problems with our president, and even sometimes, the latest episode of Star Trek.

BD: They watch TV?

AARON: I guess. They seem to know a lot about Star Trek. It's actually quite humorous.

BD: Good to know. Is there any pattern to how often you hear from them or is one particular time of the day better than another?

AARON: Not really. It's just random.

BD: During these encounters do you smell or feel anything?

AARON: I don't smell anything since the communication is mostly through psychic channels. As far as feelings, I get all warm and have a sense of safety. Almost like I am wrapped in a big thick blanket.

BD: You said mostly? What do you mean by that?

AARON: Sometimes I have dreams. I guess that is psychic too. I like to think of dreams as more intuition. I guess you could say it's the same.

BD: Got it. I know this is going to probably sound disrespectful, but I just have to ask. Are you on any medications from a doctor or anything recreational?

AARON: Not at all. I actually get that question a lot and not as nicely put. I get that it is hard to believe, but it is not chemically induced. I do drink wine, but it's more of a glass with dinner than finishing off a bottle. Beyond that, no unnatural chemicals in my body.

BD: Understood. I just want to ask. Sometimes people take medications and are not aware of the side effects. I like to check. Is there anything else you would like to share about your conversations with these aliens or the messages you receive?

AARON: No, I think that's about it. Well...uh... maybe there's just one more thing. You hear about abductions and bad things happening to people from alien beings. I think those people are in need of medical attention. The aliens are just here to help us. They are a positive influence and really shouldn't be feared.

BD: Is it not possible that there are different extraterrestrials that do harm people? Even among humans we have good and bad people.

AARON: Possible? I guess. However, I have never received a message to confirm that. If I get any other messages to the contrary, I will definitely share.

BD: I appreciate it. Thank you for your thoughts on that and I appreciate your time.

AARON: You're welcome.

NOTES:

I did hear back from Aaron about a week after this interview. According to him, he checked back in with the extraterrestrial race known as the Pleiadians and they confirmed that they don't know of any species that were abducting humans. They did confirm that they work with some people that have given their permission. I asked him to expand on that and at this time, no further details have been provided.

In the world of ufology, the Pleiadians are humanoid extraterrestrials that are sometimes called the Nordic aliens. They have been in legends for several hundred years and are believed to come from the Pleiades open star cluster. It's one of the closest star clusters to earth. The first astronomer to see Pleiades was Galileo Galilei. It can be found as the eye of the bull in the constellation of Taurus.

The identification of the Pleiadians started with Native Americans. In Cherokee legends, it is said that their people originated in the Pleiades cluster. They claim to have come to this world as star seeds to bring light and knowledge. If the stories are true, then modern day Cherokee, as well as other Native Americans, could be part Pleiadian.

ENCOUNTER SEVEN

Doctor Alien

INTERVIEWER: B.H. Daffern, represented as BD in transcript.
SUBJECT DETAILS:
NAME: Steve (alias)
AGE AT TIME OF INTERVIEW: 33 years old
ENCOUNTER DATE: April 2010
OCCUPATION: Police Officer
NOTES:

- Introductions, identity validation, platitudes, and closing statements have been removed to protect subjects identity and personal information. This may cause you to doubt the interview because of the abrupt start and end. It is by design.
- Prior to the interview, the subject was asked to submit a written account of their experience to allow preliminary investigation of their claims.
- Fillers (um, uh, basically, you know, etc.), false starts (incomplete sentences), repetitions (repeated words and sentences), and contradictions have been included.

BD: Thank you for taking the time to talk with me.
STEVE: Happy to do it.
BD: I've read through your account and would love for you to tell me about it without looking at your report. Please make sure

to include any emotions, feelings, or senses. Things you might have smelled, heard, or felt. Stuff like that.

STEVE: I just want to ask again; my name won't be shared with anyone? I could lose my job or worse.

BD: Absolutely, no one will contact you or have your information.

STEVE: Okay, good. You are going to think I'm crazy and so will everyone else. There was a guy who mentioned seeing something last year and he's not with the department anymore...anyway, what do you want to know.

BD: I read your statement and you were very detailed. What I would like is for you to tell me your story, not read it, from your best recollection and let me know what you felt, sensed, or any emotions you had.

STEVE: Gotcha. You want to verify my story.

BD: Nothing like that. I just want to bring out the feeling side of it which people tend to leave out of their stories.

STEVE: Sure. Well, first, let me tell you I don't mind saying this, but it scared the shit out of me. I was heading back to the station along Peachtree Road when I heard a buzzing. At first, I thought it was my radio or maybe the batteries were dying on my mobile unit. I checked all my equipment and nothing, not a damn thing. But that buzzing was still going. After a few minutes, it was really agitating me. My heart was racing, and I was getting pissed. I pulled over. There were no businesses around, it was the deserted patch a few blocks from the freeway. It was about one in the morning on a Sunday, so no one was out.

BD: Did the buzzing stop?

STEVE: No. I turned the car off, but it wasn't that. I checked everything in the car with a battery and still nothing. So, I got out. And if I wouldn't be damned, it was even louder outside.

BD: Were there any energy plants or telephone poles nearby?

STEVE: Nothing, that's the damned peculiar part. It seemed to be coming from all around, but a voice in my head was telling me to walk into a patch of trees nearby. It was coming from in there. Maybe it was my gut instinct or something, but I felt like I had to go in there. The closer I got to the trees, the louder it seemed to get. I didn't know what I expected to see, but it definitely wasn't aliens. (sighs). There was also this strong smell of burning. Not like a campfire, but sort of like the stove.

BD: So, like a gas range?

STEVE: Yeah, sort of like that.

BD: How strong was the smell?

STEVE: Pretty strong, but definitely didn't smell like a fire in the brush. I decide to ignore it. Steve goes silent and I have trouble hearing him breathe.

BD: Are you there Steve?

Steve doesn't respond to me for twenty seconds.

STEVE: Yeah, I'm here. I just get chocked up when I think about it.

BD: Understandable. Take a minute to catch your breath.

STEVE: Thanks. I'm good. Ok, so I came out on the other side of the trees and there was this small group of little men. I think six of them. Not midgets, but proportionately correct sized people. They had no hair, ash colored skin, and no clothes. They each did have a belt around their waist with things that looked like they could have been tools. And the butt cheeks?

BD: Butt cheeks?

STEVE: Yeah, they didn't have any. It was like they were in jumpsuits, but it was the same color as their head, so it had to be their skin. They were all leaning over something, but I couldn't see what it was. I unclipped my holster and quietly drew my weapon.

BD: Was the buzzing still going on?

STEVE: Now that you mention it, I don't think so. I don't remember it anymore. I hadn't thought about that. No. It was definitely gone. Not sure why. Anyway, I aimed my weapon and stood up. My hand was shaking so bad, I had to tuck my arm into my side to steady it. I stepped out and yelled for them to stop what they were doing and get in a line. I guess they didn't hear me or care because they didn't change. I then yelled out if they didn't comply, I would take them to the station. They all turned to me almost in synch. They had large round eyes and tiny mouths with no lips. That's strange isn't it?

BD: That description is pretty common. Have you ever watched any of the UFO reality shows on TV?

STEVE: No.

BD: Maybe read a book or two about it?

STEVE: Not really. I'm kind of dumb to this stuff.

BD: When people describe the aliens, that's how they typically describe them. But enough of that. You told them to freeze or you would arrest them.

STEVE: Yeah, and so they turned to me. It was then that I saw what they were leaning over. It was a big deer. The side of it was peeled back and two of the little fellows had instruments still stuck in its flesh. Even though they were turned towards me, their long arms were still on the tools. I asked what they were doing. None of them moved. My whole body was trembling. They weren't aggressive, but I was scared to death. My eyes were watering, my mouth was dry.

BD: How long did that stare off go on for?

STEVE: Probably a minute, but it seemed much longer. I've been on the force for almost ten years and I ain't never seen anything like that. I wasn't going to budge. After a while, one of them stepped closer to me and raised her hands.

BD: How did you know it was a her?

STEVE: Hmmm...I'm not sure. I just felt it. She had a feminine feel towards her.

BD: Interesting. Continue.

STEVE: She said something to me, that I won't ever forget. She said, "Sorry mammal, we must have left the caller on. We didn't mean for you to come this time. We only wanted the quadrupeds and not you. We thought we had it off in time. Please go back to your life. We will call you again when we need you. You are grow-ing up well." Then she stopped talking. Can you believe that shit?

BD: It is extraordinary. I have some questions, but please finish.

STEVE: I told her no problem, holstered my gun, and went back to my car. I drove to the precinct. They were worried because I hadn't answered my radio and it had been two hours since I had ra-dioed in. I argued with them that it was only ten minutes and it wasn't until they showed me the logs that I believed them. I then lied and told them that I must have lost track of time checking out a business park nearby. I wasn't going to tell them that I saw aliens. But I had a few hours missing.

BD: I understand. Anything else after that?

STEVE: Not that I can remember. But I do think someone is watching me all the time? I'm sure you want to know more. Ask your questions.

BD: Okay, I will just randomly toss them out. Thinking back, why do you think you pulled over at that specific point and time?

STEVE: I don't know. I was just so agitated, I felt like I had to. Maybe when they called me, it made me stop.

BD: And why do you think they called you?

STEVE: Because they said so.

BD: I understand that part. Let me rephrase. Why call you in-stead of someone else?

STEVE: You mean, why am I so special?

BD: Not in those words, but yes.

STEVE: I'm not sure. I will tell you I felt like it wasn't the first time.

BD: That they called you?

STEVE: Yeah. She seemed to know me. There was a familiarity there that I can't really communicate. It was a feeling, but also with her comment about me doing well. It felt like she had known me.

BD: With that point, if they had called you before and acciden-tally this time, logic says they may have called you since the inci-dent as well.

STEVE: True. I just don't know. If they did, I don't remember.

BD: You didn't know before either, did you?

STEVE: Understood. I hadn't thought about that. I don't want to think about it.

BD: Since then, have you had any missing time or some event you can't account for?

STEVE: There was one time, but I figured it was because I was drinking. So, no, nothing I can independently confirm.

BD: Were you drinking the night of this incident?

STEVE: Hell no. I'm a straight arrow. I don't drink when I'm on duty. Not worth losing my pension.

BD: Got it. Back to the location. What do you think they were doing there?

STEVE: Shit, I don't know. They were operating on the deer or something. It looked like they were digging around in it with their tools.

BD: First answer that comes into your mind. Do you feel like they killed it?

STEVE: Yes. Not sure why, but I think they did it.

BD: Can you describe any of their tools?

STEVE: They were all a shiny silver. The one that I could see clearly seemed to have a large suction cup on one side and the other looked like a swiss army knife. It had a bunch of different sized cutting tools and what looked like a vibrating rod. They had double razor-sharp edges. The one I saw that was in the deer made a bright blue light inside the cavity. Made me think of a laser.

BD: You said you were scared.

STEVE: Hell yeah.

BD: Then why did you put your gun away and leave.

STEVE: She told me too.

BD: I get it. But you are a seasoned officer, several years on the job, right?

STEVE: I am.

BD: You were seeing something going on that is obviously unusual, if not illegal. Yet, you put your weapon away and left the scene. Doesn't that seem odd to you?

STEVE: Why wouldn't I listen to her? She's in charge of (he stops) Steve goes quiet.

BD: Please continue Steve. In charge of what?

STEVE: I'm...not...sure. With this whole story, I hadn't thought about that. Why did I leave?

BD: Have you told this story to anyone else?

STEVE: No. You're the first and the only.

BD: And that part never occurred to you? Doesn't that seem strange?

STEVE: Very. I don't know why I left. I should have stayed.

BD: I have to ask. I know you said you were sober that night, but do you ever drink on the job or do any drugs? Maybe to stay awake.

STEVE: (screaming) No!

BD: Had you seen any movies or TV shows similar to this?

STEVE: No!

BD: Could you have fallen asleep in your car and just dreamed this whole thing?

STEVE: No. (he pauses) I don't think so. That would explain the missing hours and everything. Yeah, that must have been it. It was late. I could have fallen asleep. Yeah.

BD: I'm not suggesting that. I am just asking.

STEVE: The alternative to sleeping is that I met a group of aliens and mindlessly obeyed them. I think I will take the sleeping.

BD: Sorry, that is my fault. I feel like I led you there. It isn't important. What is important is you believe you encountered something and I'm going to document it. Let's switch topics. If you didn't tell anyone and it has been a while since this happened, why come forward now?

STEVE: I felt like someone should know. Someone in the precinct mentioned they had talked to you about a paranormal investigation, so I thought I would reach out and share this with you. See if you could help.

BD: I'm not sure what I can do, but I will definitely document this. Sometimes it's good just to talk to someone. There are experiencer groups that you could join to help you thru some of this.

STEVE: You mean like Alcoholics Anonymous.

BD: Sort of.

STEVE: Nope. One help group is enough for me.

BD: So, you go to AA?

STEVE: Doesn't matter? That's what that second A stands for. You have been helpful. I feel better knowing it was a dream.

BD: I'm not sure I said that. I do have a few...

STEVE: I'm tired and need to go. Thank you for your time and remember the deal, no name.

Steve disconnects the call

NOTES:

After the call, I reached out to Steve with a few more questions and to encourage him to not write this off as a dream without more consideration. He didn't have time to talk and asked me to send them in email. It has been years since that interview and even after one more reminder from me, he has not answered them. I did get an email at one point that said, it was just a dream and he was sorry for wasting my time.

The police, both in the United States and without, are bombarded by reports of unidentified flying objects. However, what is less known is they see and experience them as well. Just search for news on police encounters and you will find a diverse list of reports from credibly officers with many years of service. Some, like Steve, choose to stay silent about them. Beyond the ones that do come forward, I will always know many keep quiet for fear or ridicule.

ENCOUNTER EIGHT

Alien Round-Up

INTERVIEWER: B.H. Daffern, represented as BD in transcript.
SUBJECT DETAILS:

- NAME: Christine (alias)
- AGE AT TIME OF INTERVIEW: 71 years old
- ENCOUNTER DATE: 1963
- OCCUPATION: Postal Worker (retired)

NOTES:

- Introductions, identity validation, platitudes, and closing statements have been removed to protect subjects identity and personal information. This may cause you to doubt the interview because of the abrupt start and end. It is by design.
- Prior to the interview, the subject was asked to submit a written account of their experience to allow preliminary investigation of their claims.
- Fillers (um, uh, basically, you know, etc.), false starts (incomplete sentences), repetitions (repeated words and sentences), and contradictions have been included.

BD: Thank you for taking the time to talk with me. I've read through your account and would love for you to tell me about

it without looking at your report. Please make sure to include any emotions, feelings, or senses. Things you might have smelled, heard, or felt. Stuff like that.

CHRISTINE: You're welcome. But I am going to need you to speak up.

BD: Sorry. Without reading the email you sent me, can you please tell me about your encounter. Anything you can remember and include your feelings, emotions, and anything else that comes to mind.

CHRISTINE: Why? Can't you read.

BD: I can, but I have found that sometimes talking out loud can recall certain parts of the memory and lead to further discussions that may not have come out if it was just an exchange of written messages.

CHRISTINE: It's your nickel. My momma always told me if I was telling the truth, I didn't need to have a good memory. I know it all as if it was yesterday. Well... almost all of it. But I swear to you that I ain't lying and I know you won't believe me, but after seeing that show on the television about those things caught on tape, I just had to tell someone.

BD: I was going to ask about why you came forward now.

CHRISTINE: Yeah, it was the TV show and I've been thinking a lot about my dead brother lately.

BD: I'm sorry for your loss. Was it recent?

CHRISTINE: It's okay, he been dead for a while. Anyways. This'll knock your socks off.   It was late summer in 1963 or maybe 1964. Uh... yeah, it was 1963. My brother, Zed and I were home alone for the evening. I was 15 and he was 14. Our parents had gone out to dinner, leaving us home for the night. Zed was in his bedroom and I was in the living room watching TV. We didn't have one in every room like some kids do today and there was no internet back then, so it was the only place to watch it. It was dark out and had to be past nine since Bonanza was on. I saw something move out of the corner of my eye from outside. There was a window next to me and there was no flood light out there and the thing I saw was lighted. I went to the window to see if I could figure out what it was. Out in the field there was a bright light coming down from the sky. It hovered over the corn. I turned off the TV and the light in the room to make it darker.

BD: Why did you do that?

CHRISTINE: Not sure, why?

BD: Just curious if you felt scared or trying to hide.

CHRISTINE: Honestly, I don't remember feeling that way. I just wanted to see it better. I was excited. So, I sat there in the dark and watched, when another light came down hovering about fifty feet above the first one for just a second and then dropped below it about ten or twenty feet.

BD: How far away from the house?

CHRISTINE: At that point, not sure. But it was close. I couldn't stop watching it. I yelled for Zed. He came down cussing at me, but stopped when he saw what I was watching. A third UFO came down and followed the same path of the first two, except it lined up closer to the ground. Now there were three of them out there. Zed said we should go up on the roof to see them better. I was afraid they would fly away from us if we did. But he convinced me, and we went to my room, climbed out my window and on to the roof.

BD: Had you been out on the roof before?

CHRISTINE: Sure. All the time. Daddy and Momma would sit up there with us and look at the stars sometimes.

BD: Could you see the objects any better up there?

CHRISTINE: You bet your bottom dollar. Zed was excited. He said to me that they were about a hundred feet from us. The things...ships...whatever they were continued coming down one by one first stopping at the same place, but then moving down. They continued doing this until there was a handful of them. They then formed a circle.

BD: How many total ships did you see?

CHRISTINE: I guess it had to be nine or so.

BD: Could you hear anything or smell anything?

CHRISTINE: Not a damn thing. Not even a hum or the smell of a fart. Nothing. But I was starting to get nervous. Uh...maybe anxious. I was feeling weird. Zed and me couldn't believe what we were seeing. We didn't talk, but did look at each other a few times. I could tell that he was trying to figure what they were as much as I was. We had seen and read enough science fiction to know that they had to be aliens. They just had to be.

BD: How big were they?

CHRISTINE: I tried to figure out how big they were. I remember thinking they could only fit a normal sized man and not much more. And they would have to be sitting down, they wouldn't have been able to stand up in there.

BD: How long did they stay that way?

CHRISTINE: That's the odd part. I don't really know.

BD: How come?

CHRISTINE: They sat perfectly still, hovering in place for about five minutes, maybe more, when another ship just seemed to appear in the middle of the circle. It moved away and landed on the ground. A door opened and I saw a light on inside of it. It looked much bigger on the inside then it did on the outside. Sort of like in Doctor Who. Have you ever seen it?

BD: I have.

CHRISTINE: I could see movement inside and it looked like a lot of people. I could see them moving towards the door to come out into the field. It was at this point I broke out of whatever kind of trance I was in and realized my brother and I were alone at the house and well...I was in charge and here I was on the roof with him. I figured maybe I should be afraid, but I wasn't. Until that moment it was simply a matter of curiosity, amazement and time stood still without any sense of a threat or concern. But I decided to be afraid for him, you know what I mean? I had to protect him. We went back into my room. I looked back and one of them was coming out of the ship, it looked human from where I was, but really tall. I closed the window, went to Zed's room with him and there we sat. When mom and dad came home, we were still sitting on the edge of his bed. We didn't say a word to them.

BD: Were you afraid they wouldn't believe you?

CHRISTINE: Not really. We just didn't talk about it. This was our special sighting that was just between us. Whatever time it was after they got home, I went to bed. I looked out my window and they were gone. Just seemed more of a reason to not say anything. We did go out the next day and look around the area. We did see some footprints, but we couldn't tell if it was alien or not. It was like boots. And we never saw nothing else.

BD: Did you guys ever talk about it afterwards? Anything you might have recalled? Or did you learn how your brother was feeling?

CHRISTINE: It was a different time. I don't know how else to say it. We didn't talk about our feelings or any of that lovey dovey stuff. We were respectable children; we honored our father and mother. So, that stuff never came up.

BD: I meant no offense. I just mean did he give you any other information on how he was handling it.

CHRISTINE: A few years after that, Zed died in a car accident. He was too young.

BD: I am so sorry to hear that.

CHRISTINE: Thank you, but like I said, it was a long time ago. Until the day he died, neither of us spoke of this. After his death it occurred to me that now it was only my word of the events that took place that night. I now regret being silent. The loss of my beautiful brother was the single worst thing that had ever happened to me. This very special sighting remains just that, ours only. Which is ok, because it was for our eyes only anyway. Some things are best left alone. I know what we witnessed; I just don't know why or the meaning of this encounter.

BD: Why do you say that?

CHRISTINE: Which part?

BD: Sorry. It was meant for your eyes only.

CHRISTINE: We was the only ones that seen it. If they wanted to be seen by others, they would have shown up there. Thus, they only meant for us to see them for whatever reason. I'm tired, can we be done.

BD: Please. Do you mind if I ask some more questions?

CHRISTINE: Go ahead, but I ain't lying.

BD: I don't think you are. After the incident, did you ever feel sick in anyway or develop any type of illness?

CHRISTINE: No. I did get cancer about ten years ago, but that was from smoking. They had to take a part of my lung.

BD: You said you never told anyone before now, but did you ever have any dreams about it?

CHRISTINE: Funny you should mention that. I did. I had dreams similar to that, but they were a little off for a long while after that. I figured that was just me being scared or something. Does that mean something?

BD: Typically, it is just your subconscious trying to deal with what it saw. I am not a doctor, so I am not sure if it means anything special, but others have reported similar dreams after an encounter.

CHRISTINE: Interesting. You know...now that I think about it...Zed did come in a few times and lay next to me in bed. I asked him why and he said he had a nightmare. Maybe he was having the same ones I was.

BD: Maybe. You mentioned you were watching those shows about UFO's caught on video. Did you see anything that looked similar to what you saw and if so, do you remember what day you saw it?

CHRISTINE: I didn't see nothing like it.

BD: Would you be willing to draw something and send it my way.

CHRISTINE: I can, but I draw about as good as a pregnant yak.

BD: Doesn't have to be a masterpiece. Just your best, that would be great. Through the years have you felt the need to learn about UFO's?

CHRISTINE: No. I sort of put it out of mind until I saw that show. (pause). I guess that's about it. You want me to draw you a picture. Anything else?

BD: Just a few more things. Do you remember what the weather was like that night?

CHRISTINE: No. Why?

BD: Was it cloudy? Had it rained? Just curious if the environment had electricity in it.

CHRISTINE: Oh. No. It was dry as a bone and a clear sky. I thought you wanted to know the temperature and such. And I kept thinking why the hell would he care about that.

BD: (laugh) No... nothing like that. Anything else you can remember that seemed odd either before or after the incident? Even the smallest thing.

CHRISTINE: No. I've been thinking on this thing for a while. There is nothing else. (pauses) Our cow disappeared the next day.

BD: Your cow? What happened?

CHRISTINE: Daddy went out to milk her in the morning and she was gone. He figured somebody stole her during the night. He filed a police report and everything. We never did see her back. Eventually, Daddy saved up enough money and bought another one. That one never disappeared. I don't think it was connected.

BD: Did cows get stolen a lot back then?

CHRISTINE: Not really. I think I would know if the aliens took the cow.

BD: You were in your brothers room, weren't you?

CHRISTINE: Yes. So, I guess it's possible. But why would they steal the cow. Do they not have milk on Mars?

BD: Not sure, but it's worth thinking about. Anything else you have to share? Dig deep.

CHRISTINE: Not that I can think of. I appreciate you listening to me, even if you think I'm lying.

BD: You seem very trustworthy. I don't think you are lying. My questions are to just better understand the event. With it being so long ago, there really isn't a way to find evidence. However, I can document the best we can.

CHRISTINE: Thank you. I do appreciate you listening. It felt good to get it off my chest without you judging me.

BD: You are very welcome. If you recall anything else, please don't hesitate to reach out to me. I hope you have a good day.

NOTES:

After the call, I never heard from Christine again. She did not send me the drawing. I did reach out to her once and left a message.

The most common lore in connection with animals is alien mutilation. There are a lot of theories and reported cases in this area. What is less well known is that many more animals disappear completely in cases involving UFO's than mutilation. They just simple go away. Many theories center around natural predators, cults, or animal experiments and cruelty by human beings. There has been no proof to date of extraterrestrial abductions of our animals.

ENCOUNTER NINE

Watchers

INTERVIEWER: B.H. Daffern, represented as BD in transcript.
SUBJECT DETAILS:

- NAME: Danielle (alias)
- AGE AT TIME OF INTERVIEW: 27 years old
- ENCOUNTER DATE: Current
- OCCUPATION: Stay at home mom

NOTES:

- Introductions, identity validation, platitudes, and closing statements have been removed to protect subjects identity and personal information. This may cause you to doubt the interview because of the abrupt start and end. It is by design.
- Prior to the interview, the subject was asked to submit a written account of their experience to allow preliminary investigation of their claims.
- Fillers (um, uh, basically, you know, etc.), false starts (incomplete sentences), repetitions (repeated words and sentences), and contradictions have been included.

BD: Thank you for taking the time to talk with me. I've read through your account and would love for you to tell me about

it without looking at your report. Please make sure to include any emotions, feelings, or senses. Things you might have smelled, heard, or felt. Stuff like that.

DANIELLE: I'm just glad to get the chance to talk to you. It was very weird and has continued to be unusual. Where do you want me to begin?

BD: If you could start at the beginning and share any feelings, thoughts, and emotions. I don't want you to read the story, just tell it from memory.

DANIELLE: Sure. But first, did you send anyone over here to watch me or my house?

BD: No, I would never do that without your permission. Is there something going on?

DANIELLE: There is this car across the street with a guy sitting there. He's in black and is wearing sunglasses. Like those Men in Black movies.

BD: Maybe you should call the police and we can have this conversation later.

DANIELLE: There have been a lot of break-ins here. So, the police drive through a lot. If they thought he was a thief or something, I'm sure they would have stopped him.

BD: Well, don't confront them. If you are feeling unsafe, call the police.

DANIELLE: Hold on. I will be right back.

BD: Wait. Danielle? Are you there?

The line is quiet with the feint sound of a television in the background.

DANIELLE: (breathing heavy) He drove off and his car didn't have a license plate.

BD: That was very dangerous. What happened?

DANIELLE: I am tired of being watched. I ran out there screaming at him. His car was already running, and he drove off. I threw a rock at him and it bounced off the car. He didn't stop though. I think I've seen him before. I bet it's the government.

BD: The government? Why would they be watching you.

DANIELLE: Cause of what I saw.

BD: On that note, please take a deep breath and tell me your story. Please keep in mind your feelings, emotions, and senses.

DANIELLE: Sure. It was a few weeks ago. I took the kids for ice cream. They were missing their dad and it always helps.

BD: I was going to ask about that. Where is their father?

DANIELLE: He's in Alaska. He's in the Air Force and got stationed out there for six months for his job and training. After that, he's coming back here. We didn't want to uproot the two girls, so I stayed here with them at my Mom's and when he comes back, we will move back on base.

BD: That must be very hard.

DANIELLE: Yeah, especially with all this alien shit going on and the government watching me. Anyway, we were coming back from Dairy Queen, it was after dinner and just dark. The kids were playing in the back seat.

BD: And how old are your children?

DANIELLE: They're five and three.

BD: I love those ages.

DANIELLE: Yeah...their great most of the time. They were giving me a break and I looked out the side window and caught a fast-moving light streak past me. It was at the level of the car and about the same size. It moved fast. It was there and then gone. Never seen nothing like it. I could hear a few jets go by overhead a few seconds later. But I couldn't see them.

BD: Do you live near an Air Force Base?

DANIELLE: We don't now. My mom lives up in the mountains. But I've lived on an Air Force base and know what jets sound like, and it was definitely two of them. I was confused on what I saw, but I wrote it off as a trick of my eyes. Like maybe there was something above shining a light down on that spot as it flew by. I got home with the kids and we went inside. I left the kids with my mom and went outside to smoke a cigarette. She doesn't like smoke in the house, so there is a place on the deck I always go with a beer can as an ashtray. I had sucked down about half the cigarette when I got a chill. Like I was being watched. It was a warm evening, so it really put me on high alert.

BD: Do you remember the time?

DANIELLE: It was about nine, maybe a little earlier. It was the Friday before last, so the night was clear, but just Georgia hot. You know what I mean.

BD: Unfortunately.

DANIELLE: I stood up and crushed out the cigarette. And you know they are expensive, so I had to be feeling nervous if I wasted half a cig. I dropped it in the can and headed back indoors. Halfway in, I realized I left the butt on the deck. Mom gets pissed when I do this, so I went back to pick it up and put it in the can. That's when I saw it again. Except this time, it was higher in the sky. It was shaped like a cigar. It stretched out as it streaked by and a little bit after, two jets went by. They were pretty low which I think is illegal.

BD: About how high do you think they were?

DANIELLE: Just a little bit above the telephone poles.

BD: Wow, so pretty low.

DANIELLE: Yeah.

BD: Any idea how far away from you they were?

DANIELLE: Hmmmm... Probably out by the freeway, so maybe a mile.

BD: If you could imagine holding an object up that could black out the shape from where you were standing. How big was it? A penny, a basketball, something else.

DANIELLE: Oh. Easily a ball, maybe a baseball.

BD: Great. Continue please.

DANIELLE: I stared at the sky for a bit, but didn't see anything. I was concerned on how low the planes were flying. I went in and called the police.

BD: Did they confirm your report?

DANIELLE: Not really. They said that others had reported the cigar shaped craft and they would look into it. And that was about it from them. I kept looking out the living room window until I went to bed around midnight.

BD: According to your report, it didn't end there.

DANIELLE: Oh, no. That was just the beginning. The next night, I was sitting on the front porch with the kids and my mom. I kept looking up in the sky.

BD: Did you tell your family about what you saw?

DANIELLE: I told my mom, but she just thought I was imagining it. My best friend Becky believed me cause she is in to all that UFO stuff. She goes to the MUFON Conference in Las Vegas and all. Since we were kids, she has read and watched everything about it. Shit. I can't ever seem to get her to stop talking about it.

BD: Can I assume then that you are familiar with some of the theories and stories?

DANIELLE: Sure, some. That don't matter though. I ain't lying.

BD: I don't think you are.

DANIELLE: Just saying. I am telling the God's honest truth. We are sitting there, and a police car pulls up. Out comes one officer, a friendly looking guy and he walks up to the porch and asks to speak to me. You probably can't tell over the phone, but I'm black. We're conditioned to get really nervous when a police officer, especially a white one, asks to talk to you. Mom took the kids in and I asked him to sit down. He proceeded to ask me about what I saw the night before and what I reported.

BD: What kind of questions did he ask?

DANIELLE: Stuff about where I was and what I think I saw. He wanted to know if I was drinking or on any illegal drugs. He just assumed I was, I guess.

BD: Had you ever had any police trouble?

DANIELLE: No! Just guilty of being black.

BD: Just curious. Sorry, you have to go through that.

DANIELLE: It's okay. Racism is real, but I know that isn't what you are asking about.

BD: I had a drill instructor in the Marine Corps tell me that we were all green, just different shades. You may be dark green, I may be light green, and so on. But we are all green and it shouldn't matter what shade.

DANIELLE: I may use that. I don't think the cop was racist, he was some kind of White Asian mix, not sure. He just was very curious about the incident. Then the conversation shifted. He began to tell me that what I saw was something called ball lighting and what I thought I saw wasn't what I thought it was. Essentially, he was politely trying to change my mind. Ball lighting? You ever hear of such a thing?

BD: Ball lightning is real. However, they are typically about as big as a pea to several meters. The distance you saw it at would eliminate that. Not a whole lot is known, but it is believed to be partial compressed air and ions. I am not a scientist, but I have read up on it and it is usually only there for a few seconds and associated with thunderstorms or extreme weather. It is more sphere like. None of those seem to line up to what you saw.

DANIELLE: Yeah, definitely not what I saw. He went on trying to convince me of what I didn't see, and I think he just gave up. He thanked me for my time and then left. It was just an odd conversation. The next day, I woke up, looked out my bedroom window and saw a strange black car across the street. There wasn't anyone in it.

BD: What made it strange?

DANIELLE: No one ever parks on the street. So, it jumped out at me right away. I went about my day. I went out to the yard around lunch time and it was gone. But after that, police were driving through the neighborhood more, seems like they were always going by my house. And that car, I saw, it was the same one I just saw that sped away.

BD: You really shouldn't chase after people like that. You could get hurt.

DANIELLE: I'm tough and they should watch out for me. It was then we began to hear about robberies in the neighborhood. There was a home invasion. I don't think it is related to what I saw, just strange timing. The next night, was even weirder. I was in the shower and I could see a shadow on the other side of the curtain. It had a really large head on a tiny body. I didn't move. I just watched it until the water turned cold.

BD: Does that happen a lot? I mean the water going cold, not the shadow.

DANIELLE: After about 20 minutes it does. I didn't think I had been in that long though. I stood in the cold shower until I couldn't handle it. I looked down to turn it off and when I looked back to the shadow, it was gone.

BD: Could it have been one of your children? Sometimes shadows can expand and look different, especially if there is a lot of steam.

DANIELLE: Definitely not. They were in bed asleep. I know what this was. Plus, if the head enlarged that much, wouldn't the body?

BD: Theoretically, but I don't know for sure. So, what do you think it was?

DANIELLE: An alien. It knew I had seen it and it was coming for me. Not sure if it was just to watch me or to find out what I knew. But it was there for me. Plus, I don't know how long I was in the shower, I could have a whole lot of missing time and it could have done whatever to me. I'm not sure on the why, but I damn well know what it was.

BD: What did you do next?

DANIELLE: I got out of the shower, put a robe on and went to see if anyone was there. I walked through the whole house and everyone was in bed asleep. And you want to hear something really weird, I felt the need to look out and at that exact time, a police car drove by slowly.

BD: Sounds like a coincidence. Or do you think it meant something else?

DANIELLE: Nah, that was probably it. It was the next day that I got your name from a friend and sent you that email. Shortly after that, the phone calls started.

BD: I don't remember reading about that.

DANIELLE: It happened after I contacted you. (laughing) A lot more has happened since that night. Every so often, I am getting a phone call on my cell from an unknown number. Sometimes when my husband calls from his base it comes across as unknown, so I answer it every time.

BD: What does the caller say?

DANIELLE: Nothing really. Someone is there, just breathing. I ask who it is and then there is a loud buzz, and it hangs up.

BD: Someone could just be screwing with you.

DANIELLE: Sure, that's possible. But I don't think so. Then, there was the night before last.

BD: What happened?

DANIELLE: There was a knock on my door, and it was the police. The same guy that came by before. He asked if I could step out and talk with him. I did and he asked me if I had seen anything else weird in the sky and if I thought any more about his explanations. I wanted to scream at him, but I was really scared. Not sure why, but this kind police guy was giving me a creepy vibe. I agreed with everything he said, and he nodded. I did tell him about the strange car and that we may have had an intruder and he told me more about the break-ins. We ended the conversation and he left. Why would he come back? Doesn't that seem strange to you?

BD: For sure. That seems really odd. Out of curiosity, have you talked with anyone else about this?

DANIELLE: My husband. We talked the morning before that cop came. Officer Guy, I think he said his name was.

BD: What did you tell him?

DANIELLE: Everything. The ship in the sky, the car across the street, the weird cop visit and drive-byes. Even talked about the alien in the bathroom.

BD: What did he think?

DANIELLE: He thinks I am friggin nuts. He said something about me just being scared with him gone and that I would be better when he got home the month after next. It's not my imagination. Plus, if it was, why would the police come back again that night. The government must be listening to my calls. Maybe the aliens too. I feel like I am in the middle between the two and they are fighting over me or something.

BD: Why do you think that?

DANIELLE: They don't appear to be on the same page. But I am being watched. I don't know, I figured if they were in cahoots, they would have their shit together more. I have had a total of six phone cars, numerous drive-byes, two police visits that I know of, and it seems to all revolve around what I see. The government or the aliens, not sure which, but one of them is going to get me.

BD: Do you feel in danger now?

DANIELLE: All the time. I'm tired of it. Why do you think I chased that car? I want those shits to know I know. They are probably listening to this call. Do you hear me? I know you are listening. (silence). Maybe not. Brian, you've been asking questions, but I have one for you. What are you going to do to help me?

BD: This is an unusual one. I am not associated with any government agency or law enforcement. If you're really scared, I think you should utilize them for sure. I'm not sure what I can do, beyond sitting outside your home and being another witness. And based on what you have told me, I don't think I can do that. I'm sorry, but I will definitely document your story.

DANIELLE: You could come and spend a few nights here. I can sleep on the couch and you can have my bed.

BD: Not sure that would be a good idea with your husband out of state and I am pretty sure, my wife would have a problem with it. The optics would look bad.

DANIELLE: So, what, am I supposed to just keep watching these people watching me and listening to my calls because I saw an alien and UFO? What if that alien is doing more than just watching me?

BD: I don't have any easy answers for you. You could move and...

DANIELLE: Can't afford that.

BD: All I can suggest is don't go anywhere alone and use extreme caution until your husband comes back.

DANIELLE: That isn't helpful at all.

BD: You could set up some video cameras and if you can catch proof on tape, maybe the police or whoever you are talking to will be more willing to hear you. I'm sorry, but I really don't have much else I can do here. I really am about documenting for others. If I could do something I would.

DANIELLE: How about you call the police and tell them what is happening to me. Maybe they will believe you.

BD: Without proof, I'm not sure they would care. Plus, I don't think that will go well. Me telling them amounts to hearsay.

DANIELLE: Then I guess were done. I know I sound mad at you, but I'm frustrated. I need help and have nowhere to turn. But I do appreciate you listening. I will call you back if something else happens.

BD: You can just email me. I am on the phone a lot and probably will get it sooner.

DANIELLE: Ok, bye.

NOTES:

After the call, I received nineteen different emails. I took each email seriously and responded. They included reports of more phone calls, different cars across the street that she chased away, videos of police cars driving by her house, and even the sighting of more alien shadows in her bathroom. In reference to the alien shadows, I did get one picture from her point of view in the shower, through the curtain. She circled in yellow the shadow she saw. To my eyes, it appeared to be her shadow and I responded with that. She didn't respond to my comments. The last email I received from her was the day her husband returned from Alaska. She made a comment that since his return all activity and negative feelings were gone. She felt they were scared of him. At the time of writing this, I have not heard from her for close to six months.

The claims made by Danielle that perhaps the police or maybe the government were working with extraterrestrial beings is not a new concept. Even the theory that they are in a secret battle is an age-old conspiracy theory. The only proof that has been presented are from scientists or former military people coming out on their death beds or within financial ruin. Perhaps the most telling report was from former CIA employee and contractor, Edward Snowden. He was the man that stole and revealed many CIA secrets to the world. He would have no reason to lie. Snowden went on record claiming that he had searched the stolen secrets he had acquired and could say with a degree of certainty that the United States Government is not aware of any intelligent, extraterrestrial life. This is only one data point and tends to contradict others. I thought it important to share in relation to this story. Obviously, we may never know the truth.

ENCOUNTER TEN

You Have to See This

INTERVIEWER: B.H. Daffern, represented as BD in transcript.
SUBJECT DETAILS:

- NAME: Edgar (alias)
- AGE AT TIME OF INTERVIEW: 28 years old
- ENCOUNTER DATE: 2015
- OCCUPATION: Middle School Teacher

NOTES:

- Introductions, identity validation, platitudes, and closing statements have been removed to protect subjects identity and personal information. This may cause you to doubt the interview because of the abrupt start and end. It is by design.
- Prior to the interview, the subject was asked to submit a written account of their experience to allow preliminary investigation of their claims.
- Fillers (um, uh, basically, you know, etc.), false starts (incomplete sentences), repetitions (repeated words and sentences), and contradictions have been included.

BD: Thank you for taking the time to talk with me.
EDGAR: Sure.

BD: I've read through your account and would love for you to tell me about it without looking at your report. Please make sure to include any emotions, feelings, or senses. Things you might have smelled, heard, or felt. Stuff like that.

EDGAR: Sure. Do you want me to start at the beginning or when I got involved? Basically, stuff happened like before I got there to my friend. You know what I'm saying.

BD: I do. Yes, please start at the point you got involved. I would love to talk to your friend for his part.

EDGAR: He said he doesn't want to talk. He just wants to forget it ever happened. He's a fireman and he's afraid they would think he's nuts.

BD: I will keep his real name out of it.

EDGAR: He's just not interested.

BD: Understood. Thank you for asking him. So, please start with your involvement.

EDGAR: I got a call. It was about half past nine. But like, definitely before ten. My friend, call him John, was all excited and yelling. He said, 'you have got to come see this shit." I hung up and ran next door.

BD: Did he tell you what he saw?

EDGAR: Nah. But when your neighbor says, you have got to come see this shit, you go see that shit. Know what I'm saying.

BD: Yeah.

EDGAR: I got over there, and he was looking up. I looked up and there was like this huge triangle. It was just floating between our homes. It had three blinking lights on each of its corners.

BD: What did you make of it?

EDGAR: What do you mean? Basically, it was a UFO.

BD: Were the lights flashing in any patterns? Were there different colors?

EDGAR: Oh yeah. Definitely. They were like all flashing in unison. Each corner was basically the same. Red, green, and yellow lights brightly blinking. It was like a Christmas tree. The triangle was black, so it was kind of hard to see with the bright lights on the tips. I could see the shape barely. The whole ship seemed to be about the tips. Just the tips. (laughs)

BD: Did you hear anything? Smell anything?

EDGAR: Nothing like that. It was basically silent, and the air was like right after a thunderstorm. It was muggy, but kind of electrified and smelled like burnt tofu. You know what I'm talking about?

BD: Did it look like it had any type of propulsion or something keeping it up?

EDGAR: I'm a retired Airforce mechanic and I have been around aircraft all my life. I have never seen nothing like this. I asked John how long it had been there, and he told me about five minutes. There was no one else out but us.

BD: Do you happen to wear glasses?

EDGAR: I do.

BD: Did you have them on that night?

EDGAR: I didn't. But it didn't matter it was so huge I didn't need them.

BD: Did you have your phone on you?

EDGAR: I did. And I know what you are going to ask, but I didn't take a picture. It was like I forgot I had it or something. Basically, it didn't occur to me. And I asked John later and he didn't think to take one either.

BD: But he thought enough to call you?

EDGAR: I know weird, right? But that's what happened.

BD: What came next?

EDGAR: We just starred at it. At one point, it went invisible, but not the lights. They kept flashing. If it was like farther away, I would have probably thought it was some airplanes.

BD: How far away was it?

EDGAR: Not far, it was just above the trees in the yard. So maybe a hundred feet or so above us. It started to move, and we lost it as the lights were the only thing we saw in the distance. That was it for the ship.

BD: Had you ever seen anything like that before or since?

EDGAR: No.

BD: What was the weather like that night?

EDGAR: Clear and in the eighty's. Why?

BD: Just curious about the visibility.

EDGAR: Oh, it was visible. But that wasn't the last of this encounter.

BD: What happened next?

EDGAR: John and I followed it as it went away. We didn't talk the whole time. When it was gone, I said to him how awesome it was. It was like the coolest thing I had seen. He basically said the same thing and then we both went home.

BD: Were you scared or happy or feeling anything?

EDGAR: Nah, I was felling nothing and didn't really think about it. It was almost like it didn't happen. I went to my home and he went to his. Not a whole lot was said.

BD: Does that seem strange to you?

EDGAR: Sort of, but I think we may have been in shock or something. Of course, what came next was enough to make that seem less strange. You know what I'm talking about?

BD: I read there was more.

EDGAR: Oh yeah.

BD: What happened next?

EDGAR: I went to my house; he went to his. I remember sitting on the couch deciding on whether I should go to bed or have another beer.

BD: Had you drank many beers that night?

EDGAR: I don't drink much, but I chose to have one or maybe six that night. I can't remember. I was feeling good so more likely six. I had one more and then went to bed. I guess the next thing happened a few hours later. There was this frantic knock on my door in the middle of the night. At first, I thought I was dreaming, but when the alcohol fog cleared, I got up. I went to my front door and looked through the peep hole. It was John and he was like shaking. He banged on the door again. I unlocked it. He rushed in and pushed the door shut behind him. He pushed me out of the way, locked it, and said something like they were after him.

BD: Who?

EDGAR: The aliens. They were after him he said.

BD: Was he drunk, or could you tell if he was high?

EDGAR: John doesn't really drink or do drugs. The most he does is smoke a joint or two and since he gets his stuff from me, I know he had nothing.

BD: Were you high that night?

EDGAR: I had smoked a fat one, but nah, I wasn't high. I have like an awesome tolerance.

BD: But you had beer as well.

EDGAR: True. But I was cool.

BD: What did he do next?

EDGAR: He ran to my back bedroom and slammed the door. That was fucking strange. I went back there and tried to open the door. He had pulled the dresser in front of it. I told him to open the door and he yelled, no. I demanded it and he still wouldn't. He was like scared out of his damn mind. I pushed on the door and got the door open enough that I could squeeze my fat ass in there. He was on the bed, his legs pulled up tight on his chest, and he was rocking. I went over to him and asked him what happened. I thought he may have killed someone or owed money to a mobster. At least that are the reasons on TV. But he basically just rocked back and forth.

BD: How long did he do that?

EDGAR: Up until I started to shake him. But not before all the lights.

BD: The lights?

EDGAR: You ain't going to believe this shit, but every window suddenly was filled with like this bright light. Blinding. I tried to look out one of the windows, but it was too bright. I went into the living room, every window there had a blinding light coming in. It was like the curtains weren't even there. We were basically surrounded. It lasted a few minutes and then was gone.

BD: Could you hear anything?

EDGAR: Yeah, this time there was a repeating sound of whoosh. Sort of like a helicopter. But why would a helicopter be over my house with bright lights in every window, right?

BD: But possible.

EDGAR: Sure.

BD: How was John behaving with this?

EDGAR: He didn't seem to notice. He just kept rocking.

BD: For how long?

EDGAR: Not sure. Eventually, he snapped out of it and looked at me. I was like, dude what happened and then he told me. I wish he would talk to you, but I can't make him.

BD: I get it. Can you tell me what he said to you?

EDGAR: He said that there were five green men in his house, and they were trying to take him. I guess he woke up in bed and couldn't move. He had no clothes on and could feel them turning him over. Then, he felt a pinch between his butt cheeks and felt full in there if you know what I mean.

BD: Was he naked when he ran into your house?

EDGAR: No.

BD: Just curious, continue.

EDGAR: He said they did things to him and then laid him back on the bed. He still couldn't move while they dressed him. I'm not sure what happened next, but he said he could move again. He jumped off the bed, pushed one of them over and ran. He said they were chasing him to the front door and one of them waved a hand and it locked. He went to the open window next to the door, kicked out the screen and jumped out. He ran straight to my place and that was when he started banging on my door.

BD: Did he say anything else?

EDGAR: Not really. But I did go over in the morning to check out his house. The front door was wide open, the screen was outside on the ground, and the inside of the house was a mess. I went to his bedroom and the sheets and bedding was messed up. There was one drop of blood on the sheets, but that could have been from anything. I came back and told him his house was cleared and never heard anything about it again.

BD: So, after that night, he didn't tell anyone about it.

EDGAR: Not that I know of. I tried to bring it up a few times, but he like shut it down. You know what I'm saying. HE. SHUT. IT. DOWN. He did move shortly after that. We stay in contact which is how I got ahold of him for your request.

BD: I appreciate that. I have a few more questions that might help me research the area. Do you know if anyone else reported anything that night?

EDGAR: Actually, I was curious and started checking around a week or two after that. There was one person that had called into a radio show and I happened to catch the tail end of it when I started my car up. They had just seen a triangle ship in the area. But that's it.

BD: Did you have any changes in your health after that? Or do you know if John did?

EDGAR: I didn't, and I don't think John did, but like I said he moved away. But I don't think so.

BD: After thinking through everything you saw and experienced, what do you think that encounter was all about?

EDGAR: Basically, I think we saw something that they didn't want us to see. And maybe, they thought that like both of us lived in his house and came back to make sure we didn't talk about it. Whatever they did to him that night, shut him up.

BD: So, you think they did something to make him silent?

EDGAR: Definitely. They were tying up loose ends.

BD: So, you do believe that he was probed by aliens and escaped?

EDGAR: Sure, as shit. You didn't see him. He was out of his damn mind and not in the good way.

BD: Have you ever read or seen something on television in relation to unidentified flying objects or alien beings?

EDGAR: Oh yeah, I love that shit.

BD: Have you ever read or saw anything that would compare to your event

EDGAR: Not at all. That's how you can tell I didn't make this up. This was really weird.

BD: I appreciate that. Is there anything else you would like to add?

EDGAR: I can't think of nothing. But I will email you if I do.

BD: I appreciate it.

NOTES:

After the call, I talked with the local police about any helicopter activity in that area. Because it was five years prior to the interview, they didn't have any records to share with me. However, they assured me that they would never shine lights into a home in the manner I described, nor did they have a helicopter big enough to shine multiple lights in all the windows. They went on to explain to me that even if they had three helicopters, which they actually only have two, but if they had three, they could not fly close enough to get equal shine that bright into every window.

I never could confirm the report that Edgar said he heard on the radio show and his friend John never responded to additional inquires to talk off the record. Last I talked to Edgar, he was still living in the same place with no activity. He did add in an additional conversation that he was more sure than ever that if the things in the giant triangle knew where he lived, they would have anal probed him too. No other data has become available.

ENCOUNTER ELEVEN

Not Ghosts

INTERVIEWER: B.H. Daffern, represented as BD in transcript.
SUBJECT DETAILS:

- NAME: Frank (alias)
- AGE AT TIME OF INTERVIEW: 21 years old
- ENCOUNTER DATE: October 1998
- OCCUPATION: UFC Fighter and Student

NOTES:

- Introductions, identity validation, platitudes, and closing statements have been removed to protect subjects identity and personal information. This may cause you to doubt the interview because of the abrupt start and end. It is by design.
- Prior to the interview, the subject was asked to submit a written account of their experience to allow preliminary investigation of their claims.
- Fillers (um, uh, basically, you know, etc.), false starts (incomplete sentences), repetitions (repeated words and sentences), and contradictions have been included.

BD: Good afternoon. Thank you for speaking with me.

FRANK: I'm not going to lie. It is a pretty weird thing that happened, and you probably will think I'm nuts. But I ain't lying.

BD: Don't worry about that. I just want to hear your story as you remember it and understand what you experienced. Try to share any smells, feelings, or things you may have sensed.

FRANK: I'm not going to lie, it was a while ago, so some details are fuzzy. But here is what I can remember. I was six years old and my mom was walking me to school. I laugh sometimes thinking about little me. Now that I am buff and get in the ring to bust up opponents good, I wish the me of today could be back there.

BD: Everyone wants to protect their younger selves, totally normal. You were probably too young then to take up boxing anyway. Please continue.

FRANK: We always went the same way. Even though the sun was up, it was starting to get cold in Georgia, so we was all bundled up. We walked between two apartment complexes and down this street with a tall fence on it and then into another parking lot. The bus stop was on the other side of the lot.

BD: What was it a lot for?

FRANK: Another set of apartments. These were four stories tall. They aren't there anymore. I went back before I sent this in and was surprised to see it's a grocery store and an empty field now. The empty field behind it is still just as empty with trees. Anyway, we started across the parking lot and that's when I saw them. I'm not going to lie, even though I was six, I said shit and tugged on my mom's hand. See, the apartment had this brick wall in front of it. It was about waist high to an adult. Standing behind it were three figures. They seemed very human-like, youthful, they had curly hair and a blank stare until they noticed that I was looking at them and then their eyes widened as if they was surprised that I had noticed them observing us. Like I was not supposed to be able to see them and once me and the beings made eye contact, I had their attention. Everything on their upper torso was white with a grey tone kind of mixed in, including their faces, they were almost transparent like one would imagine a typical ghostly figure to be. I mentioned only 'upper torso' because I don't recall them having any hands or legs, including feet. They also seemed to be floating, I think. I starred at them and they just stared back. We just looked at each other.

BD: Did your mom see them?

FRANK: No. But she did say something weird to me. She said...
Frank stops talking.

BD: What did she say?

FRANK: I don't see them, Mi Corazo'n, but I have before. I have before!!! What had she seen before? That's crazy right?

BD: Did you ask her?

FRANK: It didn't really occur to me to ask about it until I was older, and she didn't want to talk about it. I could tell she didn't want me to bring it up no more. I'm not going to lie, when your moms say she don't want to talk and she looks that scared, you don't ask no more. Plus, she mostly spoke Spanish, so it was hard to understand her anyway. My brother and I were not very good at it.

BD: You have a brother? Younger or older?

FRANK: He's younger.

BD: Was he with you that day?

FRANK: No, he wasn't in school yet, so he was back home with my grandma. Dad wasn't around. He was still in Mexico or something. I never knew him.

BD: Sorry to hear that. Did you ever talk to him about it?

FRANK: I did a couple of times. He believed me and was really cool about it.

BD: Had he ever seen anything? Or maybe gave any other thoughts?

FRANK: Nah. He didn't really say he did. But he did have nightmares that would say he had. I just don't know if it was what I told him that gave him nightmares or if he got them on his own from something he saw. Just can't tell you.

BD: No worries. Let's get back to the incident.

FRANK: Yeah. So, my mom's didn't see them. There were a bunch of kids on the other side of the lot at the bus stop with parents. It didn't look like no one could see them either. I'm not going to lie; I was thinking I was nuts. We were about halfway across the parking lot and I looked back, and they were still there. They started walking towards me and they passed through the brick wall they were behind, and you know what? Those shits didn't have lower bodies. It was just the top half and they were following us. I told my Mom that they were coming, and she looked back, and I swear, she wasn't looking where they were, she was looking where they moved to and said, I don't see anyone. You should just ignore it and let's keep moving. If she couldn't see them, then how did she know they were in a different spot than before?

BD: Do you think she was lying?

FRANK: I'm not going to lie; I knew she was. Oh, she was lying, but I didn't know why. I actually said something to her, but I don't remember what. She looked at me like she was mad, and I stopped asking. Eventually, the bus came, I got on, and watched the lot as we drove away. They were still there and coming closer to my mom's. She turned and walked the opposite direction of them, and I never saw them again.

BD: What do you think they were or what they wanted?

FRANK: I've thought a lot about that. I think they wanted me. Not sure why or how, but I think they wanted me. But not in a bad way, they just wanted to reunite, you know.

BD: Why do you say reunite?

FRANK: Uh...not sure why that came out. I guess I just felt that they knew me, and I knew them, and we were friends or something. Maybe family.

BD: What were you feeling through this incident? At any point were you afraid or excited? Anything like that?

FRANK: I was scared at first like I said, but then I was more confused than anything. I think I was more afraid that my mom said she didn't see them, when it seemed clear she could. I was scared at one point when I saw they kept coming, but it went away quick. I think if I was older, I might have been more nervous. When you have aliens wanting to talk to you, that ain't normal.

BD: Is it possible they weren't aliens?

FRANK: Oh, they were. I know it.

BD: Do you remember if there were any odd smells in the air or maybe did the air seemed electric?

FRANK: Not that I can remember. If it was weird, I just didn't notice.

BD: No worries. Could the beings have been ghosts and not aliens? Sounds like a lot of what you talked about goes with paranormal reports.

FRANK: No, absolutely not! These were aliens. I know that.

BD: How do you know that?

FRANK: I can't explain it. I just do. I hear what you're saying, and I have seen ghost shows and shit, but these were not them. I can feel it.

BD: No worries, just try to be open to all possibilities. Another thought, why you? I mean no disrespect, but what made you special to them?

FRANK: I just don't know. It has bugged me. Maybe it was just my turn.

BD: Your turn? What makes you think that?

FRANK: I feel like it was just my time. Like they cycle through people and my number was up. Weird, I know. Sometimes I spend too much time in my head.

BD: Do you believe you were ever abducted by the beings either before or since?

FRANK: Shit. I certainly hope not. I don't want anything up my ass for probing.

BD: Not every abduction case is like that. You hear about those more in the media and movies because it's scarier. I have talked to folks who believe they have had perfectly nice conversations with beings from other planets. Do you think it is at least possible that you could have been abducted?

FRANK: No. I would like to think I would know if I had. I am too in control my mind and body for anyone to do anything that I wouldn't know about.

BD: Not to push too much on this, but if you felt like you knew them and it was your turn, what did you think it was your turn for?

FRANK: I don't know. Can we just forget it? I don't want to talk about that part anymore.

BD: Why?

FRANK: I just don't. Let's move on. I really don't want to talk about.

BD: Why is that?

FRANK: I just don't feel like talking about. Please.

BD: Okay. Since then, have you ever felt watched or maybe thought someone was there, but they weren't?

FRANK: Nah, not really.

BD: Not talking abduction, is there a chance that you have met with them or seen them before and just didn't remember?

FRANK: Well, if I don't remember, I can't really answer that. I'm not going lie, the more I think about it, the more I remember little details.

BD: Like what?

FRANK: Like I remembered them as three guys. But as time went on, my brain determined they were pale white, and I could see through them. Then later, that they were tall and that there was three of them. Originally, I thought there were two. It just seems that it gets more familiar all the time.

BD: That happens. Here's the big question for you. Why now? It has been just about two decades, why tell someone now?

FRANK: I'm not going to lie. I don't really know. I've been having dreams lately. Like vivid shit, you know. My brother and I are in bed and these aliens come and take him and I can't move, but we are little. Not sure if it's just bad dreams, but it made me start thinking more about it. Not sure if something is wrong, but I just sort of feel like they are back and want me again. And I am enjoying my life now, I'm fighting and winning and getting an education. You know what I'm saying.

BD: I get it. Have you ever thought about hypnosis?

FRANK: You mean like making me talk like a chicken and shit.

BD: Well, yes, but not making you talk like anything.

FRANK: I'm not sure. I don't want to be out of control. If I go under and get angry, I might start swinging.

BD: You will never be in danger or do or say anything that you are not willing to do. They can't convince you to go kill someone. The movies make it seem like they control you and make you do all these bad things. That just isn't the way it goes.

FRANK: Ah. I didn't think that stuff was real.

BD: It's true that there are arguments on both sides. Let me ask you this, have you ever read or watched any documentaries on alien abduction or any of the symptoms?

FRANK: Not that I recall. I mean I know what it is and how people joke about it, but I don't think I ever read anything fact based.

BD: That's actually good. The two sides of the hypnotic regression argument have those that believe and those that the memory may be real, but most likely it is just derived from information they gathered through things like reading, television, radio, and sources like that. If you have not read or seen much on it, that might help eliminate that. I'm not sure I completely understand it, but I know it isn't harmful. I have seen documented cases of young children recalling past lives and languages that they could not have known. So, there is something to it.

FRANK: That is weird.

BD: I know two guys in the field and if you would like to meet with them to discuss, I bet they could help you gather some of your memories back. If nothing else, they could at least answer your questions and talk through your concerns. There is no pressure. It may not work for you anyway. Not everyone can be hypnotized, but it couldn't hurt. Plus, if you don't feel comfortable after talking to them, there's nothing lost.

FRANK: I don't know. I need to ask my mom's.

BD: Of course, she can come if you want.

FRANK: Nah, she's back in Mexico. I know I'm twenty-six and I'm tough, but I would want her to tell me what she thinks.

BD: That's no problem. If you want to reach out to her and get back to me, I can help set that up. Back to your encounter. Is there anything that has come to mind while we were talking or anything else you want to share.

FRANK: I don't think so. I'm not going to lie, it felt good to tell the story. Thank you.

BD: You're welcome. You have my contact information. Let me know what you end up deciding on the regression.

NOTES:

After the call, Frank and I connected and agreed to meet with the two hypnotists I knew. We met at one of their homes and talked for a little over an hour. We set up a time for a hypnosis session and answered several regression questions. Frank's session was a little over a week later.

During the session, he went under quite easily and the questions began. Each answer confirmed what he had reported. The hypnotists went deeper. While under, he recalled in great detail being abducted on multiple occasions. The empty field behind their apartments was the place that it had happened. I did visit the location alone and could see a clearing in the middle that matched his description, but found no evidence. He went on to describe watching his little brother being abducted on similar occasions. His brother never mentioned anything before, and Frank was going to talk to him. On that, I have no further details.

There was a second session set up to dive deeper into what he experienced during the abduction. His mother had flown in from Mexico and was present for this. She was a very nice woman, but it was obvious she knew more than she was saying. I did not attend this session and even though I saw the notes, I did not conduct any interviews. The biggest thing revealed during this session was his hands. It is a common theory that individuals who are believed to be alien human hybrids will have a confusion of identities. However, while under, if you ask them to look at their hands, you can typically get the same type of response. When asked to look at his hand, Frank cited that the hand kept changing from five fingers to three big fingers and from his tan color to white to silver. As I mentioned, this has been reported by multiple individuals believing they were abducted, but prior to this, I subtly asked questions of Frank and he was adamant he was not abducted which means he would not have wanted this to come out.

Frank agreed to a third session, but never showed up. When I reached out to him, his number was disconnected. I sent him and email, genuinely worried for him. A few weeks passed, and I received a message that he packed up and moved to Florida. Even though he was doing well in the local fight circuit and in his last year of school, he chose to immediately leave. I asked why and wished him the best. I never heard from him again.

Hypnotic regression is a pseudo-science tool used in many scenarios outside of alien abductions and close encounters. Its main focus is about healing the unconscious mind such as those that have experienced a traumatic event. The experience of regressing can often be a scary proposition for the subject. Most practitioners will have the subject describe the events as if they were watching it on a movie or television screen to remove the immediate feeling of danger. At this point, there is no concrete evidence that it reveals the truth. However, it has been a successful form of therapy for some.

I believe in this case; it had been too much for Frank.

ENCOUNTER TWELVE

On the Ball

INTERVIEWER: B.H. Daffern, represented as BD in transcript.
SUBJECT DETAILS:

- NAME: Harriet (alias)
- AGE AT TIME OF INTERVIEW: 65 years old
- ENCOUNTER DATE: July 1967
- OCCUPATION: Corporate Finance Vice President

NOTES:

- Introductions, identity validation, platitudes, and closing statements have been removed to protect subjects identity and personal information. This may cause you to doubt the interview because of the abrupt start and end. It is by design.
- Prior to the interview, the subject was asked to submit a written account of their experience to allow preliminary investigation of their claims.
- Fillers (um, uh, basically, you know, etc.), false starts (incomplete sentences), repetitions (repeated words and sentences), and contradictions have been included.

BD: Thank you for taking the time to speak with me.

HARRIET: You're welcome. I just felt the need to finally tell someone about this. I was watching that Ancient Aliens show, and they were talking about orbs and stuff and I was compelled to reach out. Anxious to get started.

BD: It's interesting. The shows, although sensational in their presentation, don't always get it right, but it has definitely brought a lot of people forward. I think the best place to start would be if you could tell me about your experience, without reading it, and try to remember feelings, sensations, or anything else you sensed.

HARRIET: Sure. First, this was a long time ago.

BD: 1967, if I recall correctly from your email.

HARRIET: Yep. July 15th to be precise.

BD: How does that date stand out for you? I have trouble remembering my own birthday sometimes.

HARRIET: I remember it because it is my birthday. (laughs) I had a great day at the house. Everyone came over and being up in the mountains, it was a rager. Well... as much as it could be for a twelve-year-old girl. It ended about eight or nine at night. A friend of mine and I were going to camp in the woods next to my house. There was a small store and service station a mile to the west of my house. Our mode of transportation were bicycles. My friend had a slow leak in his front bike tire. Around eleven at night we decided to ride to the store and put air in his tire and get some snacks.

BD: What was your friends name?

HARRIET: Let's just call him my friend. I don't think it's right for me to share his name.

BD: Fair enough. So, you were heading out to the station. Seems pretty late for a trip that far for young kids.

HARRIET: Things are different in the mountains. It was pretty normal to be out and about like that. It was summer and it wasn't like we had to get up for school or nothing. I remember thinking how pissed I was that my birthday was in the summer because we didn't get to celebrate in class with cupcakes and stuff. Looking back, it seems so silly, but it was important back then.

BD: I totally get it.

HARRIET: Anyway. We were about a half a mile from my house and we saw a red light like on a plane, but it wasn't blinking, and we couldn't hear any noises and there were no other lights. We thought it wasn't moving so we stopped on our bikes. After only a few seconds it started moving north slowly. No noise or blinking still. We started back moving and a few seconds later it stopped. We went through this routine several times. It appeared it was watching us as we were it. Keeping pace with us. At least it did that for a while. Finally, it moved at a much faster pace to the north and disappeared. We made it to the store and pumped his tire up. It was at a five-road intersection. That was a busy spot for our town.

BD: Were there a lot of people out?

HARRIET: Come to think of it. No, not really. We saw a few cars roll through the stop sign, but that was it. There were workers in the store, but not sure how many. Probably around three would be my guess. We finished pumping the tire and immediately thought we may get in trouble if the police saw us out that late. We turned back and headed east toward my house. My friend looked back when we got to where the road, I lived on started and he slammed on his brakes, and hollered, "God dammit!!! Look Harriet!!!" I stopped fast and looked back. There was a big orangish yellow ball sitting there almost as low as we were, hovering. No sound. Just like a really big full moon rising, but close and just hovering still. We were looking west then I think. It seemed within no more than fifty feet away from us.

BD: Were there any other people out or cars at this point?

HARRIET: No. We hadn't seen any since the intersection. Weird. We had seen no other cars out the whole time.

BD: Is that really an unusual thing at what was probably almost midnight at this point?

HARRIET: I guess not. I just seem to remember the roads being busier than they were that night. But that could be my memory.

BD: Tell me more about the object. Did you feel anything?

HARRIET: It had two colors, orange and yellow. They were swirling inside slightly. I didn't really feel anything at all. More stunned or shocked is probably a better way to say it.

BD: Do you think it was the same red light you saw on your way to the station?

HARRIET: I think so. I mean what are the chances of seeing two spaceships in one night. With the colors swirling, I think it may have just look red far away.

BD: How about your friend? Was he feeling anything, or did he think it was the same object?

HARRIET: Maybe. I don't know. We kept talking and asking each other what it was and making comments that it was the same thing that had watched us all the way there. I don't know how long it sat there still and quiet. It was at least a minute or two. Then there was this sound, kind of like a burp and four smaller white balls of energy emerged. They came closer to us and seemed to swirl around in excitement.

BD: Why do you think they were excited?

HARRIET: Their movement seemed joyful. I guess... I guess I felt joyful and so I think they were. It felt good. We didn't move as they came closer and they were spinning around us. They were trying to say hi.

BD: How did you know that?

HARRIET: I could feel it, I guess. It's kind of hard to say. I could hear them, but there were no words. And they had different tones to what I was feeling, not hearing.

BD: Do you believe the smaller balls of light were aliens?

HARRIET: Absolutely. They didn't have bodies like ours. This was who they were. I can't remember everything they said, but we interacted with them a bit. They went back into the larger object when we finished. Absorbed I guess and then the large ball shot up in the sky about tree height and then shot out to the west. Again, no sound. Like it was there & real quickly got smaller and gone in a few seconds.

BD: Were either of you able to make out any other details about the smaller objects or the larger one before it went off?

HARRIET: Not really.

BD: Did either of you wear glasses or contacts and not have them in?

HARRIET: He wore glasses and had them on, but my vision was good.

BD: How big were the smaller objects?

HARRIET: They were about the size of us. So, kid size.

BD: Any guess on how many of them could have fit in the larger object if you were comparing them?

HARRIET: Oh, at least a hundred if not more.

BD: At this point, did either of you feel sick or weird in any way?

HARRIET: No, not that I can remember. My friend ended up dying of cancer, but that was thirty years later. We were feeling good. No fear, no pain, no anger. None of that. We were happy and excited.

BD: What did you do next?

HARRIET: We took off to my house as fast as possible. Instead of camping, we went in and woke up my parents. One weird thing is on the clock, we had been gone two hours, but to me it was no more than an hour. We lost an hour somewhere. You know, like they talk about on the shows. Anyway, we woke my parents and told them all about it. As you can probably imagine, they didn't believe us and were pissed we woke them. They thought we were making it up. My friend and I went back to the tent outside. We were there about an hour or so when my friend sat up in his sleeping bag and screamed. He wanted to go home, and he was so scared.

BD: Did he have a nightmare or something?

HARRIET: He didn't say. He just wanted to go home. I woke my parents up again and we loaded his bike in the trunk of Mama's car and took him home. They were even more pissed, but they didn't say anything. He was definitely scared out of his mind, but I didn't have any nightmares. Not sure really what happened to us.

BD: Any lasting impact to you that you may attribute to that encounter?

HARRIET: I've had bad dreams of gravity stopping & people holding me down as I was being lifted up. I have them all the time since this incident. They started a week or so after that night, but I don't wake up screaming or nothing. I even talked to a hypnotist. She said she could take me back to that night, but I said no because maybe if something happened. I didn't wanna know.

BD: Do you still feel that way?

HARRIET: Absolutely! I just don't want to know. I always look up and have seen many UFOs along with some of my friends since then, but nothing like the little ball lights we saw that night. Not sure if what I see now are moons or planets or something explainable. I feel something is missing and really wonder what, if anything, happened that night. I'm in my sixties now and was twelve when this happened. Hardly ever see the guy I was with that night, but when we do see each other his first comment is "YOU REMEMBER THAT NIGHT?" Of course, I do. We were afraid to tell anyone other than my parents.

BD: I thought you said he died of cancer thirty years after the incident?

HARRIET: No, I didn't.

BD: Let me look at my notes. Yes, I asked you if either of you feel sick or weird in any way? And you said, "No, not that I can remember. My friend ended up dying of cancer, but that was thirty years later. We were feeling good. No fear, no pain, no anger. None of that. We were happy and excited."

HARRIET: I don't remember saying that. Sorry, my mind is going. He is very much alive.

BD: Do you think he would want to talk to me?

HARRIET: He might. I will talk to him next time I see him and ask.

BD: That would be great. It will help build the account of the experience to get two different point of views.

HARRIET: I get it. I'm sorry about that brain fart. My husband died of cancer about then. I think I just got mixed up. I ain't lying though. I'm telling this story now because I wanna know what if anything happened that night. I guess I'm asking what to do? Without being hypnotized. Feel like I'm missing something. I would never make something like this up. I'm many things, but a liar is not one of them.

BD: I didn't think you were.

HARRIET: Either way, thanks for letting me tell this story. You are better than a therapist. I just need you to please advise me what to do.

BD: Well, that's the trick right. This happened over fifty years ago, so there is no evidence and near impossible to find other witnesses beyond you and your friend. The only lingering evidence could be in your memory and I totally respect your wishes to not be regressed. It looks like you get confused so it might not help anyway. Beyond that, I don't really have anything to share with you. If you have another encounter you can always call law enforcement, but the nature of these encounters makes it quite difficult to 'help' anyone. I know that isn't what you wanted to hear, but I don't want to mislead you. There are groups in some cities where people can meet that have experienced things like you have and of course there is always online to find like-minded folks. Other than talking to people, I can't really think of anything else.

HARRIET: That is exactly no help. I figured you would know of other stories and figured this all out already and you could just tell me what I experienced.

BD: (nervous laugh) I wish that was true. However, if I or anyone else had this figured out, they would be all over the news. All we can do is group together stories with dates, times, and experiences and build on each other's story.

HARRIET: It isn't a story.

BD: Poor choice of words. I apologize. I mean that only by putting the witnesses experiences together, can we further the understanding of what has really been happening.

HARRIET: I guess. I'm not sure what I expected. (pause) I just hoped there would be more answers. Thanks for your time.

BD: You are most welcome.

NOTES:

I followed up with Harriet a month after this interview. She had talked to her friend and he said that he was not interested in talking with me. It seemed odd, so I asked if she could give him my card in case, he changes his mind. She never responded to this request.

I did a lot of research in her area covering most recent times where data existed. The area of the mountains she lived in had at least one report of seeing an unidentified flying object and about every three months, the sighting of a possible extraterrestrial. However, it is important to note they also have as many, if not more, Bigfoot sightings in the same area. So much so, many Bigfoot hunting organizations organize camps in the area. It may go without saying, but there has also been no verified proof of the existence of a cryptoid in the area either. Interestingly enough, there are large groups of people that believe alien spacecraft and bigfoot have more than a passing association. Sightings of ships in the sky do seem to occur in the same place and around the same time as sightings of tall, furry, apelike beings. Is it a coincidence?

ENCOUNTER THIRTEEN

ALIEN SEASON

INTERVIEWER: B.H. Daffern, represented as BD in transcript.
SUBJECT DETAILS:

- NAME: Oscar (alias)
- AGE AT TIME OF INTERVIEW: 38 years old
- ENCOUNTER DATE: May 2011
- OCCUPATION: Sanitation Truck Driver

NOTES:

- Introductions, identity validation, platitudes, and closing statements have been removed to protect subjects identity and personal information. This may cause you to doubt the interview because of the abrupt start and end. It is by design.
- Prior to the interview, the subject was asked to submit a written account of their experience to allow preliminary investigation of their claims.
- Fillers (um, uh, basically, you know, etc.), false starts (incomplete sentences), repetitions (repeated words and sentences), and contradictions have been included.

BD: Thank you for taking the time to talk with me.

OSCAR: You are most welcome. I'm anxious to share what happened.

BD: Have you shared with many people?

OSCAR: Oh yeah. (laughs) Anyone who would listen? I feel better after talking to folks. I don't give a shit if they don't believe me. I know what happened and it was cool. You ready to hear it.

BD: Sure. I've read through your email and would like, if you could, to please share your story without reading what you sent me, paying careful attention to anything you are feeling, smelling, or sensing.

OSCAR: No worries about that. Also, I swear to my Lord and Savior that every word I'm telling you is the truth. Blessed be he that gave me this experience. It was really hot that day and I was sweating more than a whore in church. It was close to eleven at night. I was walking to my truck after hunting coyotes and hogs on a family friends farmland in the country. The darkness was at the point where I could no longer hunt, and the stars were getting covered by clouds. I thought for sure the sky was going to open up even though the rain app said it wasn't. But what the hell do the weathermen know anyway. Am I right?

BD: They are often wrong.

OSCAR: For sure. I must have been walking for about twenty minutes and I was coming out between some trees on one edge of the property and I was jolted to the ground. Just shocked from out of nowhere. Have you ever been electrocuted from a wall socket or a bulb plug?

BD: I did when I was younger.

OSCAR: It felt just like that. Your body goes rigid and different parts of your body start to tingle. My fingers and toes were twitching. I even peed myself a little.

BD: Do you see what shocked you?

OSCAR: I didn't. There didn't seem to be anything close enough to me to do that. It took a few minutes for me to get myself together and stand up. That's when I saw three pulsating objects in my peripheral vision. I watched as the lights moved across the open field. They were about a hundred yards in front of me, flashing a cool white light as they hovered over twenty-year pines. It took maybe half a minute for the objects to leave my direct line of sight as they continued east, but I could see their pulsating lights flashing dimly through the pines. Eventually, they moved into a hardwood bottom a few hundred yards away, dipping lower in the horizon, disappearing out of my view. It was the direction I had just come from and so I started back after them. Almost as soon as they left my view, I noticed a loud noise coming from the west. When I looked to my left, a low flying aircraft, flying what I would guess to be five hundred feet above the ground, darted east, seeming to follow the light's path. I believe the plane was going way too fast to be civilian, but I didn't get a clear enough view to be able to claim it was a military craft.

BD: How are you feeling at this point?

OSCAR: I'd be lying if I didn't say I was excited. I ain't never hunted aliens before. I didn't think there was a season for those. If I could bag one, I'd be famous and probably richer than King David or our president, Mr. Trump.

BD: I meant from the shock.

OSCAR: Oh. That was past. I didn't think nothing of it. I just went on after an alien head.

BD: If aliens do exist, you do realize they are living, thinking creatures that most likely travelled millions of miles or many dimensions to be there. I don't think you can hunt them like a coyote.

OSCAR: You must be a democrat or one of those queers from California. Ain't no law against it.

BD: I don't think that it is appropriate to...

OSCAR: (interrupting) I went into the woods with my gun raised. No idea what to expect. As I weaved between the wood, I saw the same three lights in the distance. They were sort of behind the trees, but not doing a good job of it. I crouched down below the pine branches. I think they were hiding in there from whatever that plane was that went over. Quietly, I moved from tree trunk to tree trunk making sure not to be seen.

BD: Could you see anything else?

OSCAR: No just the pulsating lights at this point. It was dark as shit. I kept this up for about ten minutes until I found myself maybe fifty feet from them objects.

BD: How big were they?

OSCAR: About the size of a big cow?

BD: So, a normal sized man could fit in it?

OSCAR: Oh yeah. They weren't pulsating as much as before. I took a swig from my flask. Just to calm my nerves, you know.

BD: So, you were feeling nervous?

OSCAR: Hell no, son. I was feeling damn right giddy. I was going to get me an alien. I never felt more alive. I was about to express my fifth amendment rights.

BD: I think you mean second amendment rights, but I get the message.

OSCAR: Whatever. I stepped out, aimed my Winchester model 94 at the closest flashy orb, and pulled the trigger. The thirty-caliber bullet disappeared into it. So, I fired a second time and then a third. The pulsing seemed to stop. The other two came closer and moved towards me. I fired a few more rounds into them, but they didn't stop as they were getting closer.

BD: Did you see any beings?

OSCAR: Yeah. Well sort of. Whenever they turned solid and not flashing, I could see a small slit in the middle and it looked like a pair of huge eyes staring at me. I am not sure if they were ships, I was shooting at or suits. But there was definitely something in them balls. I felt this sudden burst of fear. Must be what a hog felt like before I drove my knife in for the killing blow. I was still armed, but I got the hell out of there. This David was not going to knock down that Goliath.

BD: Where did you go?

OSCAR: I ran back to my truck. Got in and drove away. I looked back and could see them hovering at the end of the woods. They stayed just behind the trees. I never seen them or that mysterious plane again.

BD: Did you ever go back?

OSCAR: I did. The next day I went back out to that area with my friend. He didn't believe me. We walked through the same woods and there was no sign they were there.

BD: Did you go to where you shot at them?

OSCAR: We did, and I could see where my shots had splintered some trees. One weird thing was that there were signs of bullet holes to my left and right too. But I never aimed that direction. I guessed it ricocheted or something. Lucky, they didn't hit me.

BD: What did your buddy think?

OSCAR: He wouldn't want to get shot either.

BD: No, about your experience.

OSCAR: He thought it was my imagination since I was so drunk when I told him.

BD: How drunk were you when you saw them?

OSCAR: Oh, not at all. I just had a few swigs from my pick me up juice. When I got home though, I finished off a case of beer and then went driving around looking for him. I finally found him in the third bar I went too.

BD: It's amazing you didn't kill anyone.

OSCAR: Oh, I always drive extra careful when I drink. But I wasn't drunk, and I know what I saw. So that's the story. You gonna tear it apart.

BD: No, but I do have some questions.

OSCAR: Fire away.

BD: Did you happen to have your phone with you?

OSCAR: I wish, but no. I left it in the truck so it wouldn't go off and scare away them damn hogs. They can hear pretty good. Same with the coyotes.

BD: Did you ever talk to the people that owned the land or any neighbors to see if they heard or saw anything?

OSCAR: I did, and they didn't. But they told me they had seen some weird shit out there before. Just nothing that night.

BD: Did they tell you what happened or what they did see when they had?

OSCAR: According to them, they saw lights and that was it. They just went on inside and prayed for the good lord to protect them. They didn't want to get involved.

BD: Looking back on the incident, what do you think it was all about? Why were they there? Why did they come after you? You, know that kind of stuff.

OSCAR: Oh hell, I'm just a simple country boy following the way of God and singing the praise of Donald Trump. I wouldn't begin to understand that.

BD: Just guess for me. What does your gut tell you?

OSCAR: Well...ok. I think those things were hiding from the military and when I came on then and fired, they thought I was with the military. If they caught me, they would've killed me. I'm sure of that. They seemed really aggressive towards me.

BD: You did shoot at them.

OSCAR: Yeah, but it was nothing personal. No reason for them to get mad at me.

BD: You said there was nothing out there. How about just anything unusual like a bent branch or a burn mark?

OSCAR: Not really. You could go out there and check it out.

BD: It's been almost ten years so I don't think that will be helpful. How about since then? Any lasting sickness or more sightings? Anything you could attribute to that encounter?

OSCAR: Absolutely nothing. I have looked for it. I mean really looked. I go out at night and stare at the skies. I have been out to that same spot probably fifty times since that night. I just sit out there for hours, but nothing happens. I wish something would, but not yet. I will let you know if it does. This time I'll keep my phone on me and get a picture.

BD: Why do you keep going out there?

OSCAR: I feel drawn to it. I can't explain it. I guess you could say that I just feel like I am going to encounter them again. And if I do, I want to try to talk to them and understand why they're here and not shoot at them this time.

BD: So, you're curious more than anything?

OSCAR: Absolutely. It's a fantastic story and I want to...no... need to find out more.

BD: I definitely understand that. Is that why you chose to report it now?

OSCAR: Yes. I heard about you on a podcast and thought since you were local you might help me figure this out.

BD: Have you read or seen much on the subject of extraterrestrials or UFO's?

OSCAR: I have seen some, but not like everything I'm sure. I do love podcasts though and I have heard a bunch of stuff there.

BD: Have you ever come across anything that might be close to what you saw or experienced?

OSCAR: Not really. I did see a YouTube video that was close, but it was more like tiny orbs flying in some kind of pattern. Honestly, it looked more like bugs. Mine were much bigger and there was no formation to them. I'm damned curious as to what they were and hope you find something.

BD: Awesome. Last question. Is there anything more you want to share even if it isn't connected that might be helpful to my investigation.

OSCAR: Not really. But I do have a question.

BD: Sure.

OSCAR: Do you think they can visit us in our dreams or do stuff to us and we not know about it?

BD: Why do you ask? Have you been having nightmares or did something else happen?

OSCAR: No...no. Just curious.

BD: Some do believe that both are possible.

OSCAR: Thanks. I don't have nothing else to share. I think that's it.

BD: Great. The next steps involve me looking at other cases and see if I can find others that may have reported something in your area, I will talk to local law enforcement, and then dig into several other areas to see what else I can find. I will get back with you if I recover any addiontal evidence or can determine any further information for you.

OSCAR: Can't ask for more than that.

BD: Thank you for taking the time to speak with me.

OSCAR: My pleasure, sir. Have a great day.

NOTES:

No further information was discovered to help or confirm the report from Oscar. His case is very unusual and not something we normally hear in reports. The theory that aliens leave a larger ship and are among us in large glowing orbs with eye slots would tend to discount the majority of claims we receive that describe aliens appearing in strange naked bodies as opposed to mini ships. It doesn't make one more accurate than another. This report stood out more so for the differences between mainstream encounter reports.

ENCOUNTER FOURTEEN

The Hitchhiker

INTERVIEWER: B.H. Daffern, represented as BD in transcript.
SUBJECT DETAILS:

- NAME: Paula (alias)
- AGE AT TIME OF INTERVIEW: 22 years old
- ENCOUNTER DATE: April 2020
- OCCUPATION: Pre-Law College Student

NOTES:

- Introductions, identity validation, platitudes, and closing statements have been removed to protect subjects identity and personal information. This may cause you to doubt the interview because of the abrupt start and end. It is by design.
- Prior to the interview, the subject was asked to submit a written account of their experience to allow preliminary investigation of their claims.
- Fillers (um, uh, basically, you know, etc.), false starts (incomplete sentences), repetitions (repeated words and sentences), and contradictions have been included.

BD: Thank you for taking the time to talk with me. I've read through your account and would love for you to tell me about

it without looking at your report. Please make sure to include any emotions, feelings, or senses. Things you might have smelled, heard, or felt. Stuff like that.

PAULA: You're welcome. I'm a little nervous and hope I don't forget anything.

BD: Don't worry about that. And I ask that you please don't read from the email you sent me. Instead, just say what you recall and share any senses, feelings, or emotions you are feeling. Just take your time and start when you are ready.

PAULA: Ok. It sounds crazy, but I swear I'm not. This started a few months ago in April. With all of this COVID stuff, I was at home and not college. We had been quarantined and had no idea when we would go back. I guess we still don't. We had gone to the store to get toilet paper, but there was a shortage. Seemed they were out of it everywhere, even the one-ply crap. We had heard there was a store up Interstate 400 with some, so my Dad and I went for a drive.

BD: About what time was it?

PAULA: Just after dark. So maybe about seven.

BD: Were there other cars on the road?

PAULA: Maybe one or two, but for the most part it was empty. Sort of creepy and felt like those post-apocalyptic or zombie movies. But literally, no one was out,

BD: Oh, I remember. Everyone was huddled in their house. Please continue.

PAULA: We went driving to the store. Found one package of toilet paper. Seemed like a long way to drive, but it was worth it. We started to drive back. There were no cars anywhere on the road.

BD: Who was driving?

PAULA: My dad was. I was looking at my phone. All of sudden I heard him yell, shit. He was pointing out the front windshield. I looked up and he was leaning forward looking out the top of the window. I followed his eyes and saw a huge triangle shaped craft moving above us. What was weird it is was like one of those old western dinner triangles?

BD: What do you mean?

PAULA: It was triangle shaped, but the middle was air. Like someone took a long metal pipe and bent it to a triangle. It had an orange glow around it.

BD: Could you notice anything else about it?

PAULA: It was silver, but beyond the glow there were no other lights. There was no writing on it. Just dull, kind of blurry silver that seemed to swallow the light. The weirder part was I couldn't hear or smell nothing.

BD: Just curious, do you wear glasses?

PAULA: That wouldn't impact my ability to smell.

BD: (laugh). No, no, no. You said it was blurry, just curious if that was your eyes or a phenomenon of the encounter.

PAULA: I have contacts and yes, I was wearing them.

BD: Great. Could the fact you were in a moving car prevent you from detecting any sounds or smells?

PAULA: No, I put my window down and looked up to take a video with my phone.

BD: So, you have a video?

PAULA: Well...no. I can tell you about that in a minute. It was moving along slowly and didn't seem to care we were there. I didn't even feel any heat, which was weird because it was a hot day, and it wasn't so far away. I thought it would be hot because of the glow.

BD: If you could guess, how far away would you say it was?

PAULA: No more than a hundred feet. It was just above the treetops.

BD: How big do you think it was?

PAULA: It had to be about the size of two trucks on each side. Each side was the same length. So pretty big. Equilateral, I think they call it.

BD: That's right. So, it was moving over you. What happened next?

PAULA: I came back in the window and was looking at my dad. He was staring straight at the road. I told him it was definitely a

UFO. He nodded and the car sped up. He wouldn't admit it, but I could tell he was really scared.

BD: How about you?

PAULA: Not really. I was excited. Do you know how many followers I would get if I posted a video of this? I could explode. I hung back out the window with my camera to keep watching it, but it had turned and started over the trees.

BD: Just to confirm. At this point, there was still no other cars around?

PAULA: None. It was just us.

BD: OK.

PAULA: I told my dad to pull over. He complained something about it being the freeway and I pleaded. Eventually, he did it to shut me up. After we stopped, I ran out of the car and into the trees.

BD: What are you feeling at this point?

PAULA: Still excited, but worried my dad would be pissed. I could hear him get out of the car behind me. He was bitching about stopping and kept yelling for me to come back.

BD: Did he follow you?

PAULA: He did, but he recently had hip surgery from an accident in the gym. He's pretty buff. I could hear him following me, but there was no way in hell he was going to be able to keep up. I know I should have felt bad, but I didn't. Basically, I was all about getting more video. I went between the trees and came out to a field on the other side. It was still moving slowly in the same direction. I aimed my camera up and started videoing again. It was even closer than before and looked huge. Even though the middle looked hollowed out from far away, this close, it looked see through. Like there was a structure there, but just made of glass or something. I was guaranteed to get a blue check mark.

BD: Blue check mark?

PAULA: When you get over ten thousand followers on Instagram, it really tells people that you're somebody in the social media world.

BD: I did not know that. Please continue.

PAULA: I was narrating the video when I thought I heard my dad behind me. I should have been suspicious because he wasn't yelling at me. The next thing I know, I was pushed to the ground and dropped my phone. I turned over, but it wasn't my dad. It was an alien. I swear to God it was.

BD: Describe them to me.

PAULA: It was just one and I think he was a guy. But he didn't look like the aliens you hear about; he wasn't green or had big eyes. He was tall with really pale skin. He had blonde hair and blue eyes. His forehead was bigger than normal, but something else was off on his face. Maybe his eyes were too far apart. Hard to place it, but it was wrong somehow. It looked like someone tried to look human and missed some of the details. Does that make any sense?

BD: It does. Not sure if it was an alien, but your description matches that of a supposed race known as the Nordic aliens. Some call them Pleiadians or Plejaren. Anything else you can remember about him? Was he sweating? Did he have a limp? Anything human like that maybe you just take for granted.

PAULA: Nothing like that at all. Really. I mean he was breathing. I did see his chest rise and fall.

BD: Curious, could he have been human, but just a little messed up from an accident or something?

PAULA: Oh, it was alien. I don't know how to describe it, but it was. He was too much of a fake looking human to be a mutant of anything. The other weird thing is he was smiling, and his eyes felt kind. I wasn't scared. Just pissed off from being knocked down. The ground was damp and now I was wet.

BD: Do you remember what he was wearing?

PAULA: Actually, I don't recall all the details. That weird? I want to say a jumpsuit, but not sure. Whatever it was it was a dark orange. I know that.

BD: Like a prison jump suit?

PAULA: If you are talking about the ones in Orange is the New Black, then no. This was much darker. He extended his hand and said, "Sorry young female." But he didn't say it.

BD: What do you mean?

PAULA: It was in my head. His lips weren't moving. I know that sounds crazy. But here is the crazier part. It felt normal to me. It didn't even phase me. He extended his hand further down, but I didn't grab it.

BD: Why? I thought you weren't scared.

PAULA: I wasn't, but I will still uh...uh...uh... confused. Because he was off. I don't know. Just didn't want to touch him. He starred at me a bit. Not in a creepy way, just curious. Like I said, his eyes were kind. I think he genuinely was sorry he knocked me over and wanted to help me up. His hand was extended for what felt like forever. Still, I didn't take it. I shook my head and said, no. He nodded his head at me and then ran across the field into another set of trees.

BD: Was the ship still above?

PAULA: No. I looked for that next, but it was gone.

BD: What did you do next?

PAULA: I just sat there. Not exactly sure why, but I just sat there staring at the trees.

BD: How long were you there?

PAULA: I don't know. I guess until my dad came out. He was yelling things like, what the hell, you could have been killed, and I even think I heard the word idiot a few times in there. He helped me up and we started back to the car. We weren't very far away from where I was knocked down when my dad asked where my phone was. I had completely forgotten about it and would probably have left it if not for him reminding me. I guess I was in a kind of shock. We went back and looked around the field. I figured it was somewhere around where I fell. But you know what, I found it much further away. There was no way I could have dropped it that far from where I fell. I doubt I could have thrown it that far if I tried.

BD: Could you have maybe just been mistaken on where you fell?

PAULA: Not at all. There was the bent down high grass where I fell as a marker. I grabbed the phone and we headed back to the car. I didn't really say a word. I may have apologized a few times, but that was about it. When we got back in the car and Dad started driving again, I pulled my phone out. For some reason, it wasn't until that moment I realized I had the video still on it. My phone was off. When I turned it back on, it had been reset to factory settings and asking me to choose the language for the phone. When I went past the set up, it was completely wiped. The video and pictures were gone.

BD: How do you explain that?

PAULA: Not sure. My only thought was when I was knocked down, he must have zapped it with something that wiped it. Not sure what else it could have been. I told my dad, but he didn't seem to care. He wasn't talking much. Not sure if it was the spaceship or if he was super pissed at me for running off.

BD: Probably a bit of both.

PAULA: Yeah. Anyway, that's it. That is what happened. Sorry it's not more exciting.

BD: That's an interesting story. I would rather have the truth than excitement. I'm curious about a few things.

PAULA: Like what?

BD: Do you think your dad would be willing to speak with me?

PAULA: No, not at all. He doesn't want any part of this.

BD: Even if I promise to keep him confidential?

PAULA: He wouldn't. After we got home that night, he didn't want to talk about it at all and when my mom asked about it, he told her to talk to me. He didn't even want to hear about the alien. He told me it was my imagination. I mean, shit, we both saw an alien spaceship, why couldn't I have seen an alien? Right? Then last night I told him I was talking to you and he tried to convince me not to.

BD: Did he say why?

PAULA: Just that no good would come from it. We saw something we were not meant to, and we should let it go. Everyone would be better that way. And then, he shut up about it. He's a pretty stubborn guy.

BD: How about you? Why come forward with the story now if he feels so strongly that way?

PAULA: The truth is I think it's narrow minded for us to think we are alone in the universe. I want people to know about this and other happenings. I just hope that more people will come forward after every time they hear another encounter. By showing people it's okay to talk about it, we help further the conversation.

BD: Wow. Well put. Keeping the encounter in mind, what do you think was happening that day or what was it about?

PAULA: I don't know.

BD: Just guess for me. Go with your gut, first thing that comes to mind.

PAULA: Hmmmm.... I think they saw me videoing them on the road and turned away to hide. When they heard us stop, they must have dropped one of their team or crew in the trees to zap my phone. Afterwards, he ran and joined up with his ship and off they went.

BD: Interesting. How have you been feeling since then? Meaning any lasting pains, illness, emotions. Stuff like that.

PAULA: Not really. It wasn't too long ago, but I will let you know if something happens.

BD: Great and if your dad happens to change his mind, please let me know as well.

PAULA: Sure.

BD: I have four daughters close to your age and I know what they would do in this situation. Since your phone didn't have any evidence, I'm curious, did you search online for any pictures or videos from other witnesses?

PAULA: (laughs). I did. I found a lot of pictures that looked like the alien. Well...not pictures, drawings. It was the same thing I saw.

BD: Would you mind sending me one? I get what they look like, but I would like to add it to the file as a confirmation on what you saw.

PAULA: Sure, I will do it after we hang up.

BD: How about the ship?

PAULA: Yeah, I found a ton that looked like that. I think one of them was even a United States aircraft. Want me to send those as well?

BD: Please. Every little bit helps.

PAULA: Sure.

BD: Well, that was all I had. Anything further you want to add or talk about?

PAULA: No, not really. Thank you for listening. If I hear anymore, I will let you know.

BD: Even if you are not feeling any trauma or lasting impact from the encounter, there are local groups of experiencers that meet nearby. I can give you their information if you would be interested in joining them.

PAULA: Nah, not at this time. If I change my mind, I have your email. Thanks again for your time. Goodbye.

BD: Great. Have a good day.

NOTES:

The extraterrestrial that was described in this encounter is known by two names, the Nordic Alien and the Pleiadians. The first report of this type of alien being occurred in 1950. They have been featured in popular culture movies and shows sparingly. It is difficult to believe this witness would have watched or heard of those shows based on the age of the programs.

ENCOUNTER FIFTEEN

Fishing for Aliens

INTERVIEWER: B.H. Daffern, represented as BD in transcript.
SUBJECT DETAILS:

- NAME: Tom (alias)
- AGE AT TIME OF INTERVIEW: 47 years old
- ENCOUNTER DATE: October 2017
- OCCUPATION: IT Security Director

NOTES:

- Introductions, identity validation, platitudes, and closing statements have been removed to protect subjects identity and personal information. This may cause you to doubt the interview because of the abrupt start and end. It is by design.
- Prior to the interview, the subject was asked to submit a written account of their experience to allow preliminary investigation of their claims.
- Fillers (um, uh, basically, you know, etc.), false starts (incomplete sentences), repetitions (repeated words and sentences), and contradictions have been included.

BD: Thank you for taking the time to speak with me. However, your request was a little unusual. A person I worked with said you wanted to talk on the phone, but you weren't willing to send me an email or open up a case.

TOM: I don't want any kind of paper trail. I was told that you can take the information down and put it in the MUFON database.

BD: I'm not longer with MUFON. However, I could connect you with one of the people I know from the agency.

TOM: No.

BD: I assure you they are all very good and do their job well and are also completely trustworthy.

TOM: No. I have been told I can trust you and to be completely transparent, I just need to tell someone and have them let me know if I am crazy or not.

BD: I'm in no position to be your therapist. However, I would love to hear your story. I can take down the information and send it in. Let's start with your name.

TOM: I don't want to give it. No personal information.

BD: It's going to be difficult to send the case in for you without a name. Plus, what do I call you.

TOM: You can call me Tom.

BD: Okay, Tom. Just know without the identifying information, I won't be able to enter it into the system for comparison. I am happy to help and document in my records in case I hear something similar.

TOM: Question then. If my information is kept private, why do you need it?

BD: Good question. Even though the name and personal information is held private, we use it in case people try to make the same report under different names or otherwise game the system by inflating the number of reports. I'm not saying you would do that, but it is the only way for us to be sure.

TOM: Understood. I just need to stay off the grid wherever I can. Knowing all that, do you want to hear about it. I'd like to share it with you, but if you think it's a waste of time I will understand.

BD: Well, we are already on the phone. Might as well. As you tell it, could you please share with me anything you are feeling or sensing. Maybe strange smells or sounds. Stuff like that.

TOM: Sure. It happened on my birthday in 2017.

BD: What month was that?

TOM: Sorry. October 2017. Three of us were out on the lake in my friends boat. It was about four in the morning. We were getting started early on fishing and beer drinking.

BD: I'm assuming it was still dark.

TOM: Pitch black. The clouds were pretty heavy and blocking out what stars there were. We had been out there no more than a few minutes when we saw a light in the distance.

BD: Any idea how far?

TOM: I don't know, maybe a mile at first. It was coming towards us, so that distance shrank over a bit of time. We lost interest after a few minutes and went back to talking about fish. Not sure why, but at some point in the conversation I looked up and saw that distant light was a hundred yards or so away and we could see more details.

BD: What do you mean?

TOM: We could see a shape now. It looked like a flying hot dog, but without the bun.

BD: So, like a cigar?

TOM: Yeah, that's better. Like a cigar. It had white lights on each end. I tapped my buddies and they looked up and saw it. We didn't do nothing but watch. I could smell something like gas, propane, I think. There was no sound coming from it. Definitely not an airplane.

BD: Was it flying over you? Can you tell how high it was?

TOM: That changed too. It flew just above the trees and hovered over the opposite part of the lake. It lowered over the water and went into it. It sank and we could see the light get smaller and smaller until it was eventually gone. The lake is only two hundred feet deep at its deepest part so it either turned off, went into a box, or the lake is deeper than we have been told. A few minutes passed; we were just staring. Without a tug or nothing, my fishing pole went flying off the boat. They reel was dragged faster than I had ever seen across the water and then was pulled under.

BD: What do you think did that?

TOM: My guess is I caught an alien of something. I don't know anything, but that was my favorite pole. And it was only mine that was taken so the hook must have snagged something that theirs didn't.

BD: What were you and your friends doing at this point?

TOM: Just watching.

BD: Did anyone say anything or look at each other?

TOM: Not really. We just watched in silence. I think we may have looked at each other. We had had a lot to drink at that point. I think maybe we were trying to figure out how drunk we were.

BD: Did you see any other lights?

TOM: No. We stayed out there another hour or so, just looking over the edge. Nothing came back up at all and when the sun came up, we headed for shore.

BD: How big was the boat you were in?

TOM: It was about thirty feet. Not tiny, but not too big either.

BD: Do you think your friends would be willing to talk to me?

TOM: They sure would. But like me, they won't share their information. One of them is a police captain and the other is a Lieutenant in the fire department. I will give them your number.

BD: That would be great. So, anything else happen or was that about it.

TOM: Oh no, more happened when we got to shore. We tied up at the dock, gathered our stuff, and headed to the car. We didn't talk much and what we did say, was about the gear. It was almost like no one wanted to talk. Maybe we were just pretending it didn't happen.

BD: Were there any other people around? I know it was early, but maybe other fishermen?

TOM: No. No one. We got on the lake at a part not very often used. We got up to my truck. I had drove us. My truck is the only one to haul his boat. Sort of a deal we worked out. But that was the last time I would do that.

BD: Why?

TOM: All the windows were smashed in and our cell phones, which were in the center console were gone. I was pissed.

BD: Did they steal anything else?

TOM: No. But I don't think it was a criminal. It was too coincidental. I'm pretty sure the aliens did it to keep us from reporting.

BD: That seems like a bit of a stretch. What convinced you of that?

TOM: We had been going there for almost ten years and never had a problem. Beyond the coincidence, which is plenty of reason, there was other stuff. We got in the truck after I bitched and moaned and looked at the rest of the truck. It didn't start, the battery was dead. So, there we were, no phones and no working cars. The aliens were trying to keep us there. The three of us started to panic a bit, even my police buddy. We argued and debated. Finally, we agreed that the aliens were trying to stop us from leaving. So, my two buddies decided they would walk the three miles or so to the gas station and call for a tow truck. I elected to stay by the car in case the tow truck reached me before they could get back. Plus, I have bad knees and it just made sense.

BD: Did you get the tow?

TOM: Eventually the truck came out and all it took was a jump to start her up. But one other thing happened before that. They had marched off and I sat in the truck. It was pretty chilly, so I took a blanket out of the back of the cab and wrapped myself in it. Huddled up, I kept looking back at the lake. I saw movement around the boat. My first thought was it could be the guy that stole our phones.

BD: I thought you believed aliens did it?

TOM: I did, but I was open to being wrong. I quietly opened the door and got out. I went to the edge of the parking lot and got a better look at the boat. It wasn't just one person moving around, there were three. They looked like midget shadows. Two were on the boat looking around and one was leaned over on the dock looking at the side of the boat. They were talking, but it had to be a whisper because all I could hear was hushed clicking like sounds. They were searching for something. I had left my gun at home because one doesn't typically take it drinking and fishing. If I had it, I probably would have walked down there loud and proud. Don't get me wrong, I wanted to go down and confront them. I was pissed about the truck still, but I didn't want to be outnumbered. All I need is to get shot or something. It is Georgia after all.

BD: What did you do then?

TOM: I watched them for a while, not sure how long. I kept telling myself to go down and break those little shits in half. Instead, I went back to the truck and slowly pulled the door shut. I waited there until the tow truck arrived. I told my friends what I saw, and my buddy checked out his boat and everything looked okay. Whatever I saw there, was gone. Not sure what they were doing, but they had gone away and didn't seem to take anything. And that was it.

BD: Yeah, that is weird. You mentioned the sun was coming up when you guys went in and yet you still saw just shadows by the boat. Why do you think that is?

TOM: I hadn't really thought about that. It is weird? I am not sure. But listen, I'm telling the truth. Who would lie about this? Hell, if it was a lie, I would have been John Wayne and went down and beat the shit out of them.

BD: I don't think you were lying. Could it have been darker than you remember?

TOM: I guess. Yeah, maybe that's it. I do remember them as shadows though. No feathers.

BD: What do you mean no feathers?

TOM: Huh?

BD: You just said no feathers. What did you mean?

TOM: I did say that didn't I? I'm not sure.

BD: Were there birds around or something?

TOM: No, I don't think so. That just came out. Weird. I guess I just misspoke. (he sounds confused)

BD: If you had to guess, what do you think they were doing?

TOM: My guess is they were looking for evidence or something that we could use as proof they were there.

BD: So, you think their actions were all about keeping their stuff secret?

TOM: Oh, for sure. I also think they had a base under that lake, and they were worried we saw that. They had to keep it a secret.

BD: Did you ever find anything unusual in your truck, on the boat, or in the water?

Tom doesn't respond for almost thirty seconds.

BD: Tom?

TOM: Sorry. I just realized something.

BD: Please share.

TOM: In my truck and on the boat, we found large feathers. I don't know why, but I blocked that out. We found several feathers.

BD: And you said no feathers earlier. Why do you think you said that?

TOM: I have no idea. (confused). Maybe I wasn't supposed to re-member. Could they have messed with me? There were definitely feathers. A lot.

BD: You also mentioned the three shadows on the boat that were there after you walked up to the truck and were gone when you went back. Could they have gotten out a different way or was the only way past you?

TOM: They would have had to go past me.

BD: What do you make of that?

TOM: Maybe they flew. What if those feathers were from them? Could they have been bird people?

BD: I have never heard that, but anything is possible.

TOM: That must be it. I don't know why I didn't remember that.

BD: Did the three of you ever go back to the lake or do anymore investigating?

TOM: We did. A few days later we went back with one of those radar devices that also measures depth. We didn't find it was any deeper than the two hundred feet we originally though, but there were a lot of ridges and parts of the ground that were higher. We thought maybe they were structures, or something based on their radar blip, but didn't know for sure.

BD: Ever thought about diving down there?

TOM: Sort of. We talked about it, but eventually decided we wouldn't be equipped to handle it if we encountered something down there.

BD: How about health? Did you or any of your friends get sick after that or some other kind of problem?

TOM: Not sick, but I did have a nice sun burn. The only thing I can think of is I was the closest to the spaceship. It turned into a tan, so no lasting stuff.

BD: Have you guys talked about it since then or maybe told other people?

TOM: Definitely didn't tell other people. You are the first for me. As far as talking about it, not really. It comes up occasionally, but seems less and less over the last few years.

BD: Anything else you feel like telling me about that encounter?

TOM: Not really. Other than I had to replace my battery it had gone bad. Not sure if that was related to the aliens I saw or not.

BD: Yeah, that's strange though. Okay, well that's all the questions I have. Anything more you would like to share?

TOM: Nah. Thanks for listening.

BD: No worries. I do want to stress that if you change your mind about letting me put your identifying information into the secure system, please contact me. I promise it is confidential. Oh, and don't forget to give your buddies my number.

TOM: Sure thing. Have a good day.

NOTES:

First interview I ever did where I did not have to come up with an alias because he didn't want to give his name. The friends of the witness never called me. I did try to reach the witness through our mutual friend, but we never connected.

Reports of UFO's submerging under water are very common. The United States Navy have reported seeing objects both go into the water and come out. The reports are typically given the name, USO, unidentified submerged object. The reason for the designation is to separate if from the stigma of UFO's or the paranormal. Most of these reported encounters, true or not, come from reputable sources and are more often see over or under ocean waters. However, at least once a year there is a report in the United States of seeing an unexplainable craft over or under a lake.

ENCOUNTER SIXTEEN

Alien Levitation

INTERVIEWER: B.H. Daffern, represented as BD in transcript.
SUBJECT DETAILS:

- NAME: Travis (alias)
- AGE AT TIME OF INTERVIEW: 32 years old
- ENCOUNTER DATE: January 2020
- OCCUPATION: Human Resource Coordinator

NOTES:

- Introductions, identity validation, platitudes, and closing statements have been removed to protect subjects identity and personal information. This may cause you to doubt the interview because of the abrupt start and end. It is by design.
- Prior to the interview, the subject was asked to submit a written account of their experience to allow preliminary investigation of their claims.
- Fillers (um, uh, basically, you know, etc.), false starts (incomplete sentences), repetitions (repeated words and sentences), and contradictions have been included.

BD: Thank you for taking the time to talk with me. I've read through your account and would love for you to tell me about

it without looking at your report. Please make sure to include any emotions, feelings, or senses. Things you might have smelled, heard, or felt. Stuff like that.

TRAVIS: Sure. It was January. Late at night or early morning depending on your preference. I was parked on the side of my cousins house sitting in my car.

BD: Do you know about what time?

TRAVIS: Probably around three.

BD: Bigger question, why were you there?

TRAVIS: Just sitting. I had drunk a lot that night and when I drove him home, I decided to sit in my car and sober up. Thought it would be the safe choice.

BD: So, you were drinking at your cousin's house?

TRAVIS: No, I drank at the bar with my cousin. I drove to his house, dropped him off, and hung out in the car to sober up before driving home. My wife would be pissed if I came home hammered.

BD: You know that's not safe.

TRAVIS: Ok. Do you want to hear my story?

BD: Yes, please.

TRAVIS: I was laying there sleeping it off when I remembered opening my eyes and seeing myself levitating in my car in a fetal position. I was tilted to the left side just a little. My body floated out the window.

BD: Was the window open?

TRAVIS: It wasn't when I passed out...feel asleep. But it was now. I was slowly moved out the window and that is when I saw something standing a few feet from my car. It was a greyish guy with a big head. He was wearing a white lab coat. I knew it had 2 arms from the coats design, but I couldn't make out what it's lower half looked like because it was dark.

BD: If it was dark, how did you see the top half?

TRAVIS: There was a glow coming from somewhere.

BD: Like a streetlight?

TRAVIS: I guess. Not really sure.

BD: Ok. How are you feeling at this point? Any smells or sounds you could detect?

TRAVIS: I was sort of out of it. My head was pounding, but I think that was more from the drinking than anything else. I wasn't afraid though. Just amazed.

BD: That's helpful. What happened next?

TRAVIS: I closed my eyes and began singing "la, la, la, la, la, la" in a song format and a male voice joined me telepathically. He was pretty good too.

BD: What was his voice like?

TRAVIS: Sort of like James Earl Jones. You know who that is?

BD: Yes. He did the voice of Darth Vader in Star Wars.

TRAVIS: Exactly. Darth Vader was singing with me and he was in key, which was cool.

BD: How long did that last?

TRAVIS: I really don't know. It seemed pretty quick to me, but I could have zoned out. It was so relaxing, and it felt really calming.

BD: Anything else you sensed or felt? Just wondering if you felt any other emotions at all at any point.

TRAVIS: Not at all. I just felt good.

BD: You are still floating in a fetal position, correct?

TRAVIS: I am.

BD: Did you feel anyone touching you or any motion change in your movement? Maybe things moving around you?

TRAVIS: You mean like a probe or something?

BD: Well, not just that. But sort of yeah, did you have any sense of why you were there or what they were doing.

TRAVIS: Not really. I did circulate a bit, but I still stayed in the fetal position.

BD: Do you naturally sleep or curl up in the fetal position often?

TRAVIS: Never. This was something forced on me. They put me in that position.

BD: Did you try to move or stretch out of it?

TRAVIS: Not really. I didn't think of it. I felt good. If it went on too long, maybe I might have. The next thing I knew, I was moving again. And then I started floating back towards the car. I was passed through the window and then lowered back to my seat. Suddenly, I sat up in my seat and everything was back to normal.

BD: Was the window open or closed?

TRAVIS: Closed, I think. Yeah...it was closed.

BD: Do you know how much time had passed?

TRAVIS: Not really. It was light out though, so I guess a few hours must have passed.

BD: Did you notice anything else off or different?

TRAVIS: There was one thing. I later realized that there was a mark on my left arm, and I couldn't remember how I got it.

BD: What did it look like?

TRAVIS: I took a picture of it then zoomed in and it appeared to be a letter 'S.'

BD: Can you send me a copy of that picture?

TRAVIS: Absolutely.

BD: Thank you. I have a few more questions if that's okay.

TRAVIS: Sure.

BD: Why do you think they chose you? Meaning, of all the people in the world, why you in the car, on that day and time, and in the state of intoxication you found yourself in?

TRAVIS: I have no idea. Maybe they wanted to do a blood test on a drunk guy. I just don't know, but it happened.

BD: What do you think the mark was for? Why mark you? Again, with all the people in the world.

TRAVIS: Maybe I'm special. Maybe the 'S' means special. Who knows? But it happened.

BD: I don't doubt you. It's just something that I am always curious about. Why do they choose who they choose? Did you have any long-lasting impact from this encounter? Maybe sickness or something else.

TRAVIS. None that I can think of. My vision got worse. I wear glasses now. But I think that was from age.

BD: Some people report being taken multiple times. Do you think this was the first and only time you encountered extraterrestrials?

TRAVIS: I do. I would know it if it happened. I'm sure.

BD: What if it wasn't?

TRAVIS: It definitely was the only time. I would remember.

BD: Some don't, but I hear you. Just two more areas, I would like to know about. You said that the window was closed when you passed out, but when you were lifted out it was open. Then again, it was open when you came back in, but closed when you woke up. How do you explain that?

TRAVIS: Simple, they just rolled it down then up again.

BD: But if that was the case, why didn't they just open the door? Or why roll it back up after they put you back in the car?

TRAVIS: Listen, I don't know. It just happened the way I said.

BD: Lastly, have you told any others about this?

TRAVIS: A few people.

BD: Did they believe you?

TRAVIS: For the most part, sure. There are a few that laugh it off, but they're not rude about it.

BD: That's good. Why come forward now with me?

TRAVIS: Listen, I'm not proud of being drunk that night or even of being taken by aliens. I just thought people needed to be aware. You can call me crazy or judge me for being a drunk, I don't care. But what happened that night, happened. And I just want my story to be heard.

BD: Well said. I'm not judging you and even if I was, it shouldn't matter. It is very brave of you to come forward. I will definitely get your story out there.

TRAVIS: Thank you.

NOTES:

I received the picture from Travis and it indeed looked like the letter 'S' was on his arm. He had been marked by something. It was raised and red and looked more like a branding than any type of tattoo I ever saw. It would be difficult for it to have happened without his knowledge, but according to him, it did.

In ufology, marks on the body vary from dark objects beneath the skin to unexplained red marks on the stomach and everything in between. The variety is so that no real discernable patter can be determined. In the movies and television shows you will always hear about alien implants. This is typically the term used to describe physical objects allegedly placed in someone's body after they have been abducted by aliens. As with unidentified flying objects, the idea of aliens putting things in our body is found mostly in science fiction and get very little attention or credence from scientists.

ENCOUNTER BONUS

Origin Story

I'm often asked how or why I started investigating aliens and unidentified flying objects. The story of most investigators begins with them seeing an object or believing they encountered an alien. My story is a little different. I have never seen a UFO or encountered an alien. I have always been fascinated with the unknown, but mostly ghosts and cryptozoology. However, there was an encounter with another person that started me on the unexplained visitors' path. As a bonus story, I wanted to share the very first interview of sorts I had in the realm of alien encounters.

It was April of 1987, one month before my eighteenth birthday. I was driving home from a party at a campsite in the Cuyamaca Mountains near my home in San Diego. I was headed off to the Marine Corps after graduation later that year in June. However, I met a girl that night that stuck with me more than either of those two significant events.

Focused on the road, I traversed the windy path down the mountain at a slow speed through large trees in my tiny Pontiac T1000. It was a two-lane road, no streetlights, and with it being dark, I was extra careful and watchful. The radio was up loud, and I was oblivious to everything else beyond that and the road.

I hadn't seen another car or person for almost thirty minutes when just ahead I saw a woman in the road waving her arms. She was beautiful. Long blonde hair, tanned skin, cut off jean shorts, and a tank top. I slammed on the breaks and skidded to a stop next to her. I cranked my window down, but by the time it had taken to roll it down, she had moved to the other side of my car and climbed into the passenger seat.

"Can I help you?" I asked.

"I need a ride, please. It's urgent." Her body was shaking slightly. She appeared to be freezing even though the night was warm.

"Is everything okay?"

"Please just drive," she said. "I need to get to a payphone quickly."

I'm not going to lie. Having a scantily clad, beautiful girl jump into my car and need me to help her went right to my head. I pulled out and started to drive. I kept glancing over to her and she continued to look in the side mirror. It was apparent she was watching for something.

"Is someone following you," I asked, giving her my best smile.

She turned to me and glared in silence. Her eyes were wide and fear filled. Time for the big bad man in me to take over.

I added, "I can protect you."

She almost smiled, but turned and continued to look into the side mirror. I knew she could talk, but didn't seem to want to. So, we drove in silence.

Ten or so minutes later, she asked, "How close is the next gas station? I have to call the police."

"What happened? Is someone hurt?"

"You don't know me. Why would you care? You wouldn't believe me anyway," she said, waving her hand at me.

"Well, let me introduce myself. My name is Brian, what's yours?"

"Ashley."

"Nice to meet you, Ashley." I tried to keep my tone positive. "It's a beautiful night, isn't it? You can almost reach up and touch the stars from the mountain."

She turned to me, her mouth slightly parted, and then she turned away. The young me was not very intuitive, and even

though I could read body language, I was not very good at interrupting it. In retrospect, it was a mixture of anger and disbelief.

"You are really beautiful," I said. "Are you single?"

She glanced at me again. The look on her face was pure terror
now. She seemed to be getting worse. It was not my finest moment. All of a sudden, this hot girl in my car didn't seem as cool or
as lucky as I thought. It was clear that she required real help, and it
wasn't my arms around her. I hate awkward silence, so I decided to
speak up, "It's about ten minutes more. They have a whole bank of
payphones there."

"Sorry. Not interested," she whispered.

It took me a moment to realize she was answering my statement
before the last one. "Hey, no problem. Can't blame a guy for trying
to date above his class."

She chuckled. A genuine laugh. She stared at my eyes and
seemed to be searching for something. I'm not sure how long it
was, but soon she spoke. "I saw an alien."

"An alien?" I asked. "You mean from Mexico?"

"No, not an illegal alien, one from up there." She pointed up.

"Ohhh," I said, fighting back a smile. I was not the brightest at
that age. "From space? Like in the movies."

"I told you that you wouldn't believe me." She turned back to
the mirror.

"Hey, sorry. Just caught me off guard. I believe you. You look
terrified. Something had to do that. What happened?"

She took a deep breath and said, "My boyfriend and I were back
at the lake. We were sitting on the beach. He was pointing out the
stars while I kissed his neck."

My first thought, shit, she isn't single. I drifted off for a moment
while she described why they were there. I kept thinking about her
kissing his neck. It was a short amount of time before I figuratively
smacked myself back into reality. My first words were a little different than those thoughts. "Where is he now?

"I don't know. He pushed me away and I looked up at him, pissed. I was feeling horny and he was turning me away. 'Look,' he yelled, and I followed his arm to his hand and then to his finger. Over the lake was a giant UFO. I mean like the size of a house and at least one story tall."

"I bet that was cool."

"No, you dumbass, it wasn't cool," she yelled back. "It was fucking terrifying. It was just hovering there watching us. He was excited and I was scared out of my mind. He said it was probably just a military test or something. But I never saw a plane like that."

The naval air station was nearby, so I could see why he would have thought that, but I still didn't say anything. My young man's brain was trying to manage this UFO story with a horny, hot girl in my car. I won't lie. It was a difficult dilemma.

She continued, "It was shaped like a triangle. It has some words on the bottom, but I couldn't read them. I begged Mike to leave. He seemed to be in some kind of daze. He was just starring at it. I shook him and it didn't help. He was still hypnotized or something. I was afraid to look at it because I thought it would do the same to me. I didn't want to be memorized."

I know that she meant mesmerize, but I let it go. "Should we go back and get him? Maybe I can help wake him up."

"No," she yelled. "Keep driving. We can't help him."

"Why? What happened?

"I started to go up the small hill to our car and get away from the water. If he wasn't going to stop looking, I was going to get in the car and go get the police. I knew immediately that it was going to hurt me if I stayed. I've seen enough movies to know that UFO encounters never ended well for humans. I didn't want no anal probe or anything."

Damn. My mind was back in the gutter. Damn it. I just nodded and said, "Dude, what'd you do next?"

"I ran to the car, but there was something new. I could hear humming coming from the lake and there was a smell. Sort of like a campfire. You know the wood burning smell. I stopped thinking maybe I should go back, but I was too scared. I jumped in the car and started it up. Mike always left the keys in the ignition, so that was the easy part. I put it in gear and hit the gas pedal, but nothing happened."

"Was the car maybe not in gear?"

"It was in gear! I'm not stupid. I know how to drive a damn stick. I tried each gear, including reverse. The car would not move. Then the lights on the dash and radio started flashing and blinked out. The engine died, and when I tried to restart it, the damn thing just clicked. The battery was dead or something. If it was the alternator, I would have still had a radio and lights."

She knew about cars, too. This was indeed the perfect woman. Even then, I hated myself for being a teenage boy with teenage thoughts. Again, thoughts and words were different. "So, what did you do?" She swallowed hard. Her mind was reliving the event. "I popped the hood and went to check the connections of the cables. Sometimes they can come off or corrode. But before I could put my head under the hood, I saw them."

"Them? The cables?"

"No. The five aliens. But they didn't look like no ET. They weren't cute and squishy. They were bone-thin with big round heads. I couldn't see any details because they were in the shadows of the trees. I didn't wait for them to even move. I ran. It seemed like a long time and then you found me."

Silence hung between us. I didn't know what to say. I was thinking she was crazy, but what I said was, "Wow. That sounds harsh, dude."

"Harsh? Harsh?!! I knew you wouldn't believe me." She crossed her arms and looked to the side mirror.

"I didn't say I didn't believe you. You are obviously shaken up by something. There are always strange things going on. They say bigfoot is out in these woods, too."

"It wasn't no damn bigfoot or bigfeet or whatever, asshole. It was aliens. Did you not hear anything I told you?"

"I heard you. Just a lot to take in, you know. It's a gnarly tale." The gas station lights were ahead on the road. "Look, there's the phones."

"Thank God," she said. "Just let me out over there."

"Hey, listen. You want me to hang out and wait with you. Maybe I can..."

"No," she interrupted. "Thank you for the ride, uh, uh..."

"Brian."

"Yes, Brian. Sorry. It's better you don't get involved." She gave me a half-smile.

I pulled the car to a stop in the parking lot. "How about I give you my number. You can call me if you need anything else."

"That's nice, but no thank you." She opened the door and ran to the phone bank.

I sat in my car and watched her. She was screaming into the phone; her arms were flailing, and her body was constricted and tense. Obviously, she was telling her story, I recognized some of the same movements and looks on her face. I was going to stay even though she didn't want me to, but I didn't want to be one of those creepers. She had a rough day with whatever happened; she didn't need to worry about me. Reluctantly, I drove off and never saw her again.

In 1987, the internet was not what it is today. We didn't have cell phones widespread, and where they existed, they weren't smart by any means. The only way to get news was the newspaper, radio, or television. For the next week, I read every page, listened every time I was in the car, and watched every show. I didn't see or hear anything about missing kids, UFOs, or a crazy mountain woman.

A few times over the years, I drove to the place where I believe I had picked her up. It was dark that night and hard to tell. I would go to the lake, but never saw anything that remotely resembled a UFO. Even though my actions were mostly driven that night by my teenage hormones and lack of pride, it was the day that I became interested in the UFO and Alien phenomenon.

THE GOLDEN RULE

After reading each of the sixteen accounts, you are probably wondering what happened with each of the reporters. Did they continue to experience things? Did they find logical explanations? Or maybe, did they seek medical care? The sad answer is we may never know. As an investigator of these types of encounters, we rarely find the answers that the victims are seeking and even more rare, hear about their lives afterward. We become authors of their stories and, similar to this book's intent, ensure people know that they are happening. Closure is never truly found. Each path leads to more questions. In retrospect, I wish there were additional questions I thought to ask or specific threads I pulled harder on during these interviews. Unfortunately, the talks weaved in different directions. I'm not sure any additional questions would have brought them closer to closure. Still, missed opportunities to dig deeper will always bother me. If you find yourself screaming at this text, why didn't you ask about X or Y? I sympathize.

The next thing that may be on your mind is how can I prove to you that these people are real and that I actually talked to them. Who's to say I didn't just make all of this up. On this topic, I have nothing to offer you but my word and these questions: As a credible investigator, why would I make up things that had no true ending? If I was going to make something up, wouldn't I offer tales that would make you think the way I do or frame a way to feel? The reality is that each of these people are indeed real, and you will never know them. The protection of their identities and their lives are of paramount importance to me. They are scared and, in some cases, in jobs that would be lost if this came to light. To that point, there have been police officers I know fired because they reported encounters with unknown aircraft or alien beings. They may hide it in another action, but that event is the impetus of the termination. I cannot and will not lead to these victims' additional suffering by shining a light on who they really are. That may cause you to not believe a word I have written, and I am okay with that. Hopefully, just reading these will open your mind to other things that might be happening in the world around you. If it makes you feel better to think of these as "Based on True Stories" events since I changed their identifying information, then please do so. These were real people.

As with any other collection of interviews from people believing they encountered aliens, some found it hard to answer my questions or perhaps were trying to fool me. Either way, I have collected several of these misstarts and questionable interviews in Appendix A of this book. It will give you a good idea of what I encounter during interviews. You would think that anyone willing to report an encounter would want to be taken seriously. Still, the honest truth is that on every excellent interview, there is at least one bad one or a hoax. It is unfortunate, but expected. Most of the time, they are easy to spot because the reporter doesn't include many details.

In the opening chapter of this book, I mentioned that I needed facts to believe. As you may have found out through reading these stories, they are very light on facts to support each encounter. In some cases, logical explanations are more believable, but the reporter is insistent that they are not the answer. On the contrary, the witnesses believe it could only be extraterrestrial. So why did I put my name to this if there are no facts? I submit to you that the entire book is filled with facts. Keep in mind, I shared with you that this was a book about belief, and from each of these interviews, hopefully, you can agree that they believed in their encounter. From that point of view, it is very factual.

There are many more stories like these out in the world. Some may lead to me publishing a follow up to this book. I leave you with one thought. If you encounter people with this type of event or any event that they are struggling to share, talk to them, keep an open mind, and be a friend. Always remember the Golden Rule: Treat others as you would like others to treat you.

FINAL MESSAGE

If you or someone you know believe they have encountered an Unidentified Flying Object (UFO) or an Extraterrestrial Being (ETB), please don't let them suffer. Almost every city has a group or organization that will listen and, in some cases, even offer a survivors group to talk through the trauma and lasting effects. Don't stay silent. Talk with someone.

Write to me at brian@briandaffern.com if you would like to share your story or receive a suggestion on possible organizations in your area for help. I promise you will remain anonymous.

APPENDIX A

ENCOUNTER MISHAPS: Missed Interview Opportunities

These interview attempts were short and sweet. They didn't go as well as I had hoped, and I often wonder if they were attempts to prank me or something deeper. I have separated them below by title. As with the other interviews, please assume the following for each one below even though it may not be listed out individually.

INTERVIEWER: B.H. Daffern, represented as BD in transcript.

All names listed are aliases for the witnesses.

NOTES:

- Introductions, identity validation, platitudes, and closing statements have been removed to protect subjects identity and personal information. This may cause you to doubt the interview because of the abrupt start and end. It is by design.
- Prior to the interview, the subject was asked to submit a written account of their experience to allow preliminary investigation of their claims.
- Fillers (um, uh, basically, you know, etc.), false starts (incomplete sentences), repetitions (repeated words and sentences), and contradictions have been included.

ENCOUNTER

Wanna Be

BD: Thank you for taking the time to talk with me.

INGRID: You're welcome.

BD: The details you listed were very vague. I need you to go in much more detail beyond your email. Not sure if it was cut off or something. All I got in the message was, I was taken into a space craft. If you could, please share your story without reading it, paying careful attention to anything you are feeling or sensing.

INGRID: Sure, but first, a question for you. Have you ever heard of Betty and Barney Hill?

BD: I have.

INGRID: Great. So, what happened to them, happened to me and in the exact same spot. My family knew them, and it was almost identical.

BD: Please share your experience as if I don't know that story.

INGRID: So, you don't know it.

BD: I do, but I don't want to skew your story or otherwise influence you. Plus, we may know the details differently and I don't want to assume anything. Is that okay?

INGRID: I guess. My husband Arte and me were driving home after a vacation from Niagara Falls. We lived in New York just like the Hills.

BD: The Hills actually lived in New Hampshire.

INGRID: Same thing. Anyway, it was in September at ten thirty and we saw this bright point of light in the sky. It was just below the moon on the horizon. At first, I thought it was a falling star, but it got bigger and bigger. I told my husband to stop the car. We had to walk our dog anyway. It had been a while since we last stopped. We had some binoculars, so I looked up through them while he walked Pooter and I could see this weird craft with lots of flashing lights.

BD: What did you husband think?

INGRID: I yelled to him to come look. He gave it a glance without the binoculars and said he was sure it was an airplane. That was until is suddenly changed direction. He quickly figured out it was not a plane.

BD: Why is that?

INGRID: It was coming right at us. We got in the car and drove away from it quickly. It kept following us. It had to be at least about forty feet long. It came down in front of the road before us and it forced us to stop.

BD: I thought you said it was behind you. How did it get in front of you?

INGRID: It was just there. I saw it. It couldn't have been more than fifty feet away. That was when they took us.

BD: Ok. I have to stop you there. You are outlining the story of Betty and Barney Hill exactly as it was reported. The chance that you would be experiencing the exact same....

INGRID: I guess you are just closed minded. I should know better than to try and boost your abduction numbers. I have heard you guys like to keep that stuff secret. You're just a government puppet. I've seen the X-files. I'm not stupid.

Ingrid disconnects the line.

NOTES:

Apparently, the woman I was talking to thought she could gain fame of some sort. When I sent her and email after this, she told me that she didn't want to talk and would be reaching out to a television station. One interesting part was that she claimed that no matter how hard I tried; I could not silence her. I offered to talk to her again and she never responded.

ENCOUNTER

Stoned Alien

BD: Thank you for taking the time to talk with me. I have read through your email and would like if you could please share your story without reading it, paying careful attention to anything you are feeling or sensing.

JACK: Uh, is this being recorded.

BD: No. I'm taking notes to capture your words, but there isn't anything I am recording.

JACK: That's good. Dude I am so high. I must have finished a whole bowl in the last hour. How are you doing?

BD: I'm fine. Should we go ahead and reschedule this. It may be hard to recall certain details if you are intoxicated.

JACK: About what?

BD: Your encounter with aliens?

JACK: Oh man. (laughs) I was high when I sent that in to you. I just wanted to talk to you. So, how many aliens have you talked to? Did Obama really go up to that secret moon base?

BD: I'm going to just go ahead and end this. Unfortunately, I have other interviews to conduct. I do appreciate your time.

JACK: Wait though, man. Do you know if the aliens ever get high?

BD: Have a good night, Jack.

ENCOUNTER

Change of Heart

BD: Thank you for taking the time to talk with me. I have read through your email and would like if you could please share your story without reading it, paying careful attention to anything you are feeling or sensing.

KELLY: I'm sorry to have wasted your time, but I have changed my mind on talking about it.

BD: Why is that?

KELLY: I just have.

BD: I'm sorry to hear that. Sometimes people think that we are going to take your information and give it to the news media or your place of work. I take the protection of your identity and the information you share with me very serious. I will never use your name, or any other identifying factors in telling your story.

KELLY: It's not that. But thank you for sharing that with me.

BD: Then may I ask what it is. If it was something I did, maybe I could find someone else for you to speak with.

KELLY: NO!!! It isn't that. They knew I was going to talk to you. They took me last night and said that if I shared any details of my encounter with you, they would hurt me again and there wasn't anything I could do about it.

BD: Who took you? You should reach out to the police if you....

KELLY: The aliens you idiot. The aliens threatened me, and I am not going to the damn police. I don't like to get slapped around. Thank you, but no thank you.

Kelly disconnected the line.

NOTES:

I have never been able to confirm an actual case of any kind of retaliation against a witness that has spoken with me from a human or anything else. It doesn't mean it doesn't happen, but I have no proof. This woman was terrified when she spoke with me. I decided to not press the issue any further.

It is important to note that many witnesses do change their mind after filing a report. Some do so out of fear, concerned they will be ridiculed or called a liar, and others just don't want the attention. Contrary to popular belief, many people are not reporting to gain fame or to try and pull a fast one. That has happened, but in my experience, a hoax or prank is very rare. When it does happen, it makes itself known. See the following story as a prime example of this.

ENCOUNTER

Alien Star

BD: Thank you for taking the time to talk with me. I have read through your email, but before we start diving in, I just wanted to let you know that I looked at the pictures you attached and even tried to flash the dark areas with light, but I could not see anything in them. Do you have the originals? Or if digital, maybe the memory card.

LEEANN: I don't have those. I download the pictures before I wipe the card.

BD: Understood. What exactly was I looking for?

LEEANN: One picture had their ship in it and the other was the head of the alien coming out from behind the tree. Maybe I just see in a different spectrum of light than you do.

BD: Uh. Uh. I don't think so. All humans can see in a certain spectrum of light. To put it a different way, the human eye can detect wavelengths from 380 to 700 nanometers. While animals like cats and dogs can see differently.

LEEANN: Do you wear glasses?

BD: I don't

LEEANN: I do. I bet that's the reason. How's your hearing?

BD: It's fine. I think this should be going the other way.

LEEANN: Have you ever seen an alien?

BD: Not sure why that's important. I should be interviewing you.

LEEANN: Fine go ahead. You like to be in charge? Tell me about my eyesight.

BD: Uh... It isn't important for now, I just wanted you to know that I couldn't see what you did in the pictures. I will show them around and see if I can get some different takes. There are a few people I know with more enhanced software and perhaps they will find more in the images than I can. Let's focus on your story. Can you share with me what you encountered, please don't read the message, just share it with me and include any feelings or sensations you might have?

LEEANN: Don't I need to sign anything first? Like a release or something.

BD: Not at all. As I said at the beginning (omitted from interview script) I will keep your identity a secret and ensure your anonymity.

LEEANN: I'm not sure what that word means. Anonymity?

BD: It means I will keep who you are a secret.

LEEANN: What if I don't want that?

BD: What do you mean?

LEEANN: When you put me on TV, I want my name known. It will help my modeling career and I am trying to get an acting job as well. Maybe a movie. A real-life alien abduction victim in a horror movie. It will be awesome.

BD: I'm sorry, we don't do that. We log your story and look for others to collaborate. We are about looking for scientific explanations for your experience.

LEEANN: Oh yeah, I totally get it. But if it helps me along the way too, then what does it hurt?

BD: Nothing I guess, but we are not connected to any of the television shows and when they do use one of our cases, which is rare, it has to be something special.

LEEANN: What kinds of things make it special?

BD: I would be happy to discuss it after the interview, but I would prefer not to share those details until after I have your story. I wouldn't want anything I say to you to influence your experience.

LEEANN: I will include whatever you want if it will help it get on TV.

BD: Just your story would be fine to start.

LEEANN: Unless we can figure out how to guarantee my story will make it to TV, I really don't think I should share it.

BD: Understood. We are about science here and trying to help those in need. Thank you for your time, but I don't think we can help you.

  LEEANN: But wait? I have a great story. It will blow your mind.

  BD: Is it true?

  LEEANN: Mostly.

  BD: No, thank you.

  LEEANN: Your loss, bye.

ENCOUNTER

Alien Eye for the Shy Guy

BD: Thank you for taking the time to talk with me. Your story is very different than anything I have heard before. I have read through your email and would like if you could please share your story without reading it, paying careful attention to anything you are feeling or sensing.

  NICK: Sure.

  Nick goes silent.

  BD: Great, go ahead.

  NICK: Ok. Nick goes silent.

  BD: Please share from the beginning.

  NICK: There is this huge alien eye that follows me around.

  Nick goes silent.

  BD: Can you please elaborate? When did you notice it?

  NICK: I saw it one day.

  BD: How did this happen? What were you feeling? Were you happy, upset, scared?

  NICK: Sure.

  Nick goes silent.

  BD: There were a few questions in my last statement. I'm going to need you to interact with me here, Nick. I threw a few things out there to talk about. Can you please elaborate?

NICK: Yep. Understood.

Nick goes silent.

BD: There is no need to be nervous. Would you prefer to schedule another time? Or is there anything I can do to help you be more comfortable. I would love to hear your story, but I can't tell you your story based on the paragraph. You need to share with me.

NICK: I understand.

Nick goes silent.

BD: I'm sorry Nick, but unless you are willing to work with me here, I don't see this interview going much further. Do you want to talk to me?

NICK: I do.

Nick goes silent.

BD: Ok. You seem like a nice guy Nick, but when you think you can open up and talk with me, I would love to talk with you. However, until then, I will file your case, but I can't really make a determination or find similarities if you won't talk. I hope you understand.

NICK: Ok. Have a great day.

Nick disconnects the line.

NOTES:

Nick and I did connect via email about a month after this. He apologized profusely and asked if we could do the interview by email. He had a condition called Selective Mutism. It is a condition in which a person normally cannot speak in specific situations or to specific people if triggered. Selective mutism usually co-exists with social anxiety disorder.

Although unorthodox, I did send him a list of questions and he answered them. I then sent him a series of follow up questions which he answered quickly as well. I would have loved the chance to hear him describe it and cross exam certain topics, but the most important thing for him and me was documenting the encounter.

APPENDIX B

UFO Shapes

The shapes of Unidentified Flying Objects, or UFO's, are as unique as the sightings themselves. Recently, the Ufology communities have been calling UFO's, UAP's, which stands for Unidentified Aerial Phenomena. They do this to help separate from the stigma associated with the use of UFO. There are a few other names that tend to get interchanged with UFO for the same reason. In addition to the previously mentions UAP, there is anomalous aerial vehicle (AAV) and unidentified aerial system (UAS.)

No matter how you refer to them, the objects come in many shape and sizes. Below is a list of the most commonly reported shapes.

- Boomerang
- Bullet
- Chevron
- Cigar
- Circle
- Cone
- Cross
- Cylinder
- Diamond
- Disk
- Egg

- Fireball
- Oval
- Rectangle
- Sphere
- Square
- Star
- Teardrop
- Triangle
- And variations or combinations of the above.

Even though this is a book about encounters or close proximity to aliens. Only nine percent of UFO encounters exist within one hundred feet of the witness. Regardless of the shape of the object, most sightings are shapes in the sky over one mile away. The second most significant number of sightings are from five hundred feet to a mile away from the witnesses.

The best-known sighting of a UFO happened in Roswell, New Mexico. In the summer of 1947, a local farmer found piles of strange debris in a pasture and immediately reported it as a UFO. The Roswell Army Air Force Base responded and claimed the wreckage was from a weather balloon. It has been thought of as the greatest coverup of a downed spacecraft while others believe it was an experimental aircraft. There are many views and details that support both sides. However, in the 1990's, the government released a report revealing the crashed object was not a balloon as they previously stated, but a surveillance craft part of the top-secret operation called Project Mogul. There are still some that believe it is just a more elaborate cover up. What the real truth is we will most likely never know.

APPENDIX C

Areas of Sightings/Encounters

Sightings and Encounters with UFO's/UAP's and alien lifeforms occur all over the world. The tracking and investigations tend to be more centric to the United States with the top three states being California, Florida, and New York. However, many other countries, both with their own government reporting centers and/or global reporting agencies like MUFON, have occurrences every day. Below is a list of countries that have witnesses reporting experiences.

- AUSTRALIA
- BELGIUM
- BRAZIL
- CANADA
- CHILE
- COLOMBIA
- CZECH REPUBLIC
- DENMARK
- FRANCE
- GUATEMALA
- HUNGARY
- INDIA
- INDONESIA
- IRAN
- IRELAND

- LEBANON
- MEXICO
- MOZAMBIQUE
- NEW ZEALAND
- NORWAY
- PORTUGAL
- RUSSIAN FEDERATION
- SERBIA AND MONTENEGRO
- SLOVENIA
- SPAIN
- SWEDEN
- THAILAND
- TURKEY
- UNITED KINGDOM
- UNITED STATES
- VENEZUELA

APPENDIX D

Have I been Abducted?

I must first site the source to this information as witnesses and reports from those that claim they were taken by beings from another planet.

Encounters with extraterrestrials that lead to abduction often starts when the person is very young. It has also been called Close Encounters of the Fourth Kind. Most cases involve victims learning of these actions in their adult life and remembering the events from their childhood. As to what the spark to their memory that brings this all back, it varies between individuals.

The witnesses don't agree on whether the experience is scary or happy or even what actually happens to them during these abductions. It is believed that the events are difficult on the physical mind and that causes the victims to push the events deep down and interrupt them in different ways that vary on the spectrum between positive and negative. This has been proven in victims of human abduction, so it stands to reason that it is possibly true with alien lifeforms. Forgetfulness is a defense mechanism that delays the knowledge, but at some point, it does come out.

The reports of the abduction experience have many similarities. Most begin in the home at night, often in bed or in a car near their home. There is an intense blue or white light, a buzzing sound, anxiety and fear or joyfulness and calmness, and the sense of an unexplained presence. A craft with flashing lights is seen and the person is walked or floated into it. Once inside the craft, the person may be subjected to various medical procedures, often involving the removal of eggs or sperm and the implantation of a small object in the nose or elsewhere. Communication with the aliens is usually by telepathy. The abductee feels helpless and is often restrained or paralyzed in some way. Experiencers often recall clear and great details about one aspect of the abduction and confused on the other parts. The only odd thing that most every report agrees on is that the aliens description aligns with the Gray type. They are four feet high, a slender body and neck, a large head, and slanted almond eyes. There is very little variety from abductees.

Here are some signs that you may have been taken by extraterrestrial beings. Although, I am presenting this a bit tongue and cheek, these are the similarities in most abduction cases. I outline these as common elements in abduction cases.

- Dreams of being in space craft or future looking ships.
- Dreams of being abducted.
- Unexplained missing time.
- Sleep disorders.
- Waking up during the night with odd body feelings such as dizziness, paralysis, disorientation, or numbness.
- Unexplained marks on your bodies.
- A bump under the skin similar to a piece of lead. It has been reported that you can remove it just beneath the skin.
- Feeling of being watched
- Sleepwalking
- Blood on your pillow or sheets with no visible source

Abduction by aliens is a real belief among many people. Some believe it should be treated as a psychological disorder. It has received its own phobia name, alienophobia. It isn't taken very serious though. Whether real or not, there are people who are afraid to sleep at night.

Brian Daffern has over thirty years in the investigation of UFO and paranormal phenomenon.

His life has been spent studying the unknown and trying to understand its deepest, darkest secrets. He has done this as a personal investigator, a paranormal field team member, a field investigator with the Mutual UFO Network (MUFON), and most recently, a State Director for MUFON.

He is a well-educated Marine, a senior leader at a well-known technology company, and a member of the Scientific Coalition of UAP Studies. He is a student of the unknown on a quest to educate and help those faced with the challenge of explaining the unusual things they believe they have encountered.